MATH ADVENTURES

A Key to Academic Math Advancement

GRADE 3

_____

_____

_____

Author: Ace Academic Publishing

Ace Academic Publishing is a leading supplemental educational workbook publisher for grades K-12. At Ace Academic Publishing, we realize the importance of imparting analytical and critical thinking skills during the early ages of childhood and hence our books include materials that require multiple levels of analysis and encourage the students to think outside the box.

The materials for our books are written by award winning teachers with several years of teaching experience. All our books are aligned with the state standards and are widely used by many schools throughout the country.

Prepaze is a sister company of Ace Academic Publishing. Intrigued by the unending possibilities of the internet and its role in education, Prepaze was created to spread the knowledge and learning across all corners of the world through an online platform. We equip ourselves with state-of-the-art technologies so that knowledge reaches the students through the quickest and the most effective channels.

For inquiries and bulk orders, contact Ace Academic Publishing at the following address:
Ace Academic Publishing
3031 Village Market Place,
Morrisville, NC 27560, USA
www.aceacademicpublishing.com

ISBN: 978-1-962517-10-2
© Ace Academic Publishing, 2023

Introduction

About the Book

Welcome to "**Math Adventures - A Key to Academic Math Advancement**"! This workbook is specifically designed to align with the school curriculum and help students improve their analytical and logical thinking skills. With over **750 questions and several word problems**, this book aims to cover all the required syllabus for students in Grade 3.

Our workbook is an excellent resource for end-of-the-year state tests given by schools, as well as a great review book during the summer. Whether you are looking to improve your math skills or simply keep them sharp, "**Math Adventures**" provides a comprehensive and challenging set of problems to help you achieve your goals.

Our authors have extensive experience in teaching and developing math curricula for students at all levels. **They have carefully crafted each problem to challenge students and help them develop key problem-solving and critical thinking skills.** The book covers a wide range of topics, including arithmetic, algebra, geometry, and data analysis, providing students with a well-rounded education in math.

We believe that with practice, anyone can master math. "**Math Adventures**" is designed to help students build confidence in their abilities and develop a love for the subject. With clear explanations, helpful hints, and detailed solutions, this book is an excellent tool for anyone looking to improve their math skills.

Thank you for choosing "**Math Adventures - A Key to Academic Math Advancement**". We hope that you find it useful and enjoyable!

Common Core Math Workbooks

 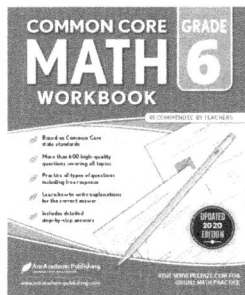  

Common Core English Workbooks

The One Big Book Workbooks

Math Adventures Workbooks

 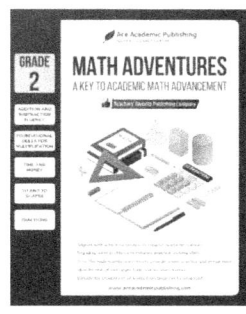  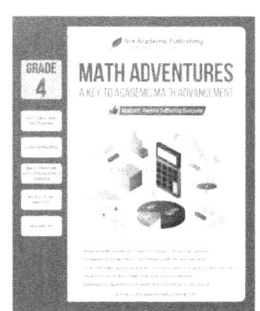

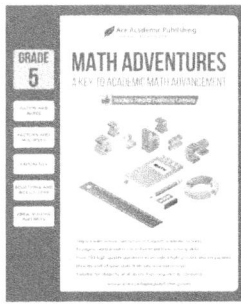 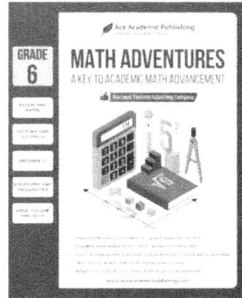 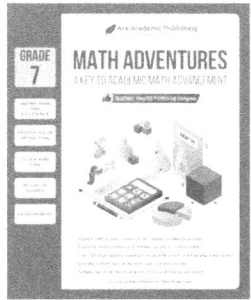 

Early Learning Workbooks

TABLE OF CONTENTS

TABLE OF CONTENTS

CHAPTER 1

MULTIPLICATION AND DIVISION

COMPLETE THE PATTERN

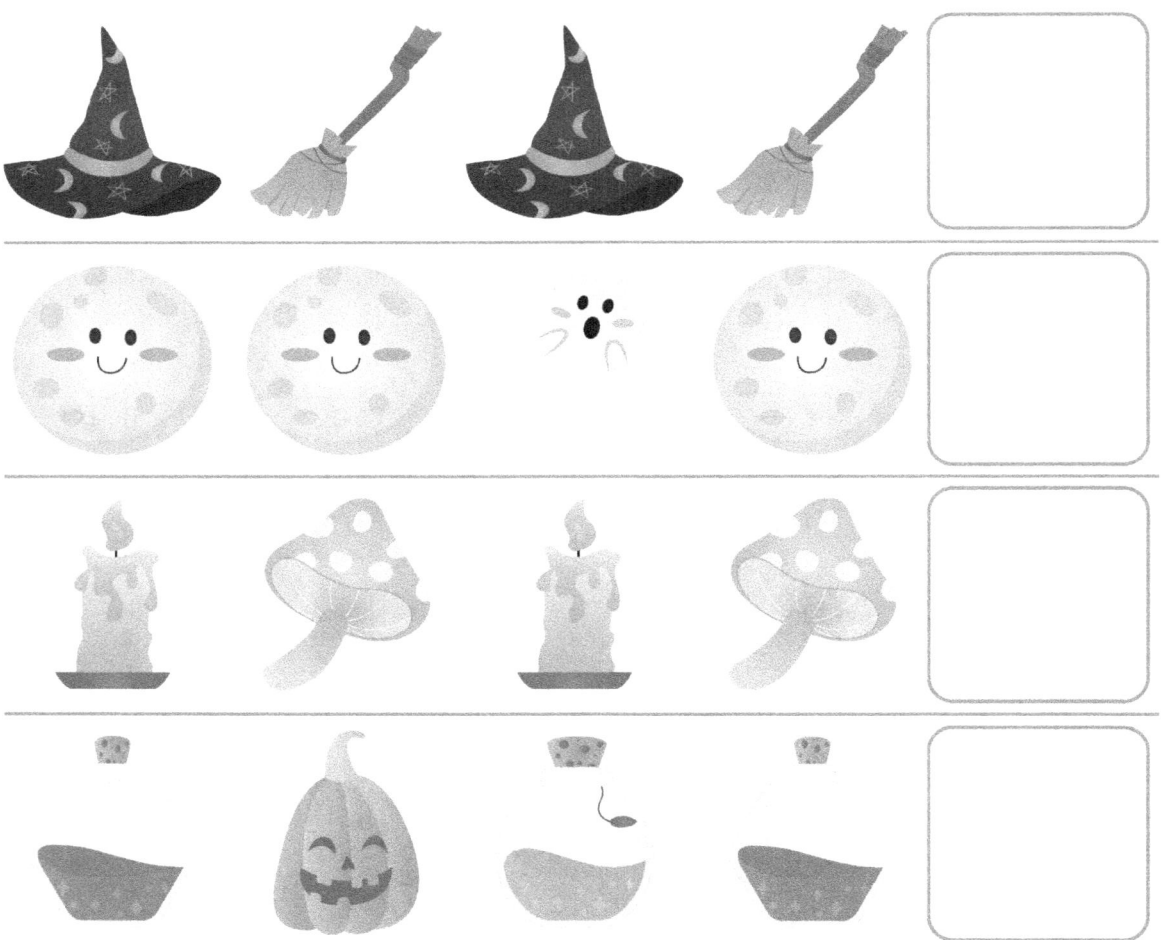

INTERPRET PRODUCTS AND QUOTIENTS OF WHOLE NUMBERS

Interpreting products and quotients of whole numbers means understanding the relationship between the numbers that are being multiplied.

The picture shows 2 groups of 3 ice creams.

Here, the total number of ice creams can be calculated by two methods.

1. Repeated addition = 3+3 = 6
2. Multiplication = 3×2 = 6.

MULTIPLICATION AND DIVISION

1.1   **Interpret Products and Quotients of Whole Numbers**

1 Complete the addition number sentence and related multiplication number sentence.

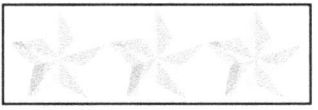  

_____ + _____ + _____ = _____ .

_____ X _____ = _____ .

2 Count the shapes and the number of groups and fill in the boxes.

_____ groups of _____ .

3 Complete the addition number sentence and related multiplication number sentence.

☐ + ☐ + ☐ + ☐ + ☐ = ☐

☐ × ☐ = ☐

(A) 2+2+2=6; 2×3=6

(B) 2+2+2+2=8; 2×4=8

(C) 2+2+2+2+2+2=12; 2×6=12

(D) 2+2+2+2+2=10; 2×5=10

4 Circle the correct number of images in each group as indicated. 6 groups of 2.

5 The picture below shows two groups of triangles. Does the figure show 3×4? Explain the answer.

(A) Yes, the below figure shows 3×4.

(B) No, the below figure doesn't show 3×4.

6 The picture below shows two groups of triangles. Does the figure show 2×5. Explain your answer.

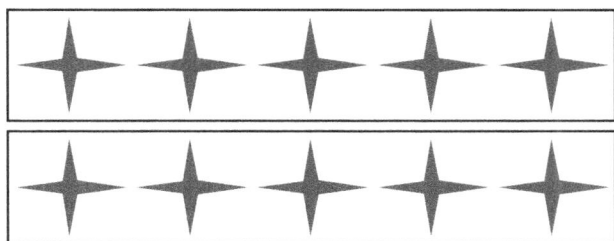

(A) Yes, the below figure shows 2×5.

(B) No, the below figure doesn't show 2×5.

7 There are 7 days in a week. How many days will be there in 11 weeks?

(A) 70   (B) 77   (C) 71   (D) 75

MULTIPLICATION AND DIVISION

1.1   **Interpret Products and Quotients of Whole Numbers**

8 Which additional equation can be used to count the total number of lemons in this picture?

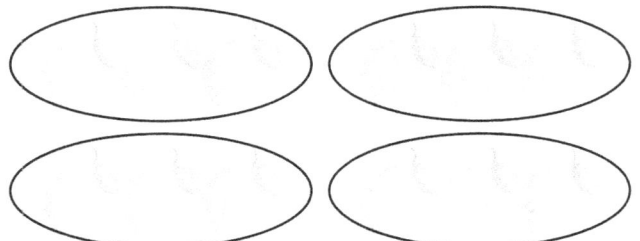

A) $3+3+3+3 = n$

B) $3+3+3 = n$

C) $4+4+4 = n$

D) $4+4+4+4 = n$

9 There are 30 days in a month.
How many days will be there in 2 months?

A) 80   B) 90   C) 70   D) 60

10 Max makes breakfast for his brothers. He makes 10 pancakes. If each of the brothers gets 5 pancakes, how many plates will he need?

A) 50   B) 2   C) 15   D) 5

11 There are 30 cars in the parking lot. If they are divided into 6 groups, how many cars are there in each group?

A) 24   B) 15   C) 36   D) 5

12 Helen had 5 boxes of pencils. Each box had 20 pencils in it. How many pencils did Helen have in total?

A) 15   B) 25   C) 100   D) 4

13 To start a card game, 48 cards are dealt equally to 8 players. How many cards does each player get?

(A) 6   (B) 56
(C) 126   (D) 40

14 There are 4 spiders spinning webs under a porch. Each spider has 9 legs. How many legs do the spiders all have together?

(A) 5   (B) 13
(C) 10   (D) 36

15 Travis made 64 pastries for a party. She invited 8 people for the party. How many pastries will each person get if she shares equally?

(A) 54   (B) 8
(C) 10   (D) 2

16 Mia has 6 boxes of pencils. Each box has 9 pencils. Which expression represents the total number of pencils Mia has altogether?

(A) 6×9   (B) 6÷9   (C) 6+9   (D) 9−6

17 Cruz has 20 apples. He wants to divide them equally into 4 baskets. How many apples will be in each basket?

(A) 24   (B) 4   (C) 5   (D) 16

MULTIPLICATION AND DIVISION

18 Jenny has 18 comic books and 24 coloring books. She places them in equal stacks on her bookshelf. Her bookshelf has 7 shelves. How many books are in each stack?

_____

19 Cooper uses the model below to write the multiplication expression 4 x 3.

Then he writes a related addition expression: 3 + 3 + 3 + 3.

Is he correct or incorrect?
Explain your reasoning: _____.

20 Merlin bought 3 packs of gum with 7 pieces in each pack. John bought 4 packs of gum with 5 pieces in each pack. Who bought more gum?

_____

Next Section:
Multiplication Within 100

MULTIPLICATION WITHIN 100

Multiplication within 100 refers to the ability to multiply two numbers between 1 and 100 to get a product. Multiplication within 100 is a foundational skill for future math concepts, such as division, fractions, and algebra.

Example:
To find the product of 2 and 12
$2 \times 12 = 24$

MULTIPLICATION AND DIVISION

1.2   Multiplication Within 100

1   Nick buys 5 bags of apples. Each bag has 12 apples. How many apples does Nick have?

(A) 70   (B) 60   (C) 75   (D) 65

2   If a week has 7 days. How many days are there in 14 weeks?

(A) 98   (B) 85   (C) 75   (D) 67

3   Paul sells donuts. He has 23 boxes of donuts. Each box has 3 donuts. How many donuts does Paul have in all?

(A) 81   (B) 87   (C) 65   (D) 69

4   Anna wants to buy 4 flowers for her sisters. Each flower costs $17. How much does Anna have to pay the flower shop?

(A) $79   (B) $68   (C) $62   (D) $75

5   Sam had 6 boxes of pencils, and each box had 14 pencils. How many pencils did Sam have in total?

(A) 84 pencils   (B) 75 pencils

(C) 82 pencils   (D) 78 pencils

6 Mark invites his friends to his house. He decides to prepare snacks for them. He wants to make cupcakes for his friends. He decides to make 4 for each person. If he is having 16 friends over, how many cupcakes should he make?

(A) 61   (B) 68   (C) 64   (D) 69

7 There are 37 swings in the park, and 2 children play on each swing. How many children are playing on the swings?

(A) 77   (B) 74

(C) 78   (D) 79

8 Emma is setting up brownies on the table for her birthday party. She organizes the brownies into 8 rows, with 12 brownies in each row. How many brownies are on the table in total?

(A) 96   (B) 78   (C) 89   (D) 69

9 Luna is buying candy at the store. He buys 11 bags of candy for $7. How much will it cost in total?

(A) $66   (B) $77   (C) $68   (D) $72

MULTIPLICATION AND DIVISION

Multiplication Within 100

10 13 cars carry people to the mall. Each car has 4 seats. How many people can the cars carry to the mall?

(A) 82   (B) 71   (C) 69   (D) 52

11 Lucas is playing six games with his friends. If each game lasted for 16 minutes and they played. How long did Lucas and his friends play games?

(A) 98   (B) 108

(C) 96   (D) 101

12 Jack goes to the zoo with his parents and his two sisters. If a ticket costs $16, how much does the family spend on tickets?

(A) $98   (B) $80   (C) $95   (D) $81

13 Mike draws strawberries on the blackboard in 7 rows, and each row has 13 strawberries in it. How many strawberries did Mike draw?

(A) 98   (B) 80

(C) 91   (D) 79

14 If a square park is 9 meters per side, calculate the area of the park.
(Given: Area of a square = side x side)

(A) 81 square meters   (B) 89 square meters

(C) 78 square meters   (D) 93 square meters

15 Emily's parents are having a party for her birthday. They are inviting friends and family over. She decides to make 2 glasses of milkshakes for each guest. They invited 6 friends and 18 families. How many milkshakes did she need to make?

(A) 48   (B) 59   (C) 42   (D) 57

16 Daniel and John are brothers. They were playing tennis. Daniel wins 7 times as many games as John. If John wins 8 matches, How many matches did Daniel win?

(A) 63   (B) 61   (C) 59   (D) 56

17 Elaina is working to improve his garden. She wants to plant 5 rows with 15 plants in each row. How many plants are there in total in the garden?

(A) 81   (B) 75   (C) 78   (D) 83

18 Ivy saved $3 per day for 14 days. How much money did she save in 14 days?

(A) 42   (B) 49   (C) 51   (D) 53

MULTIPLICATION AND DIVISION

1.2   Multiplication Within 100

19   Oliver delivers 15 deliveries a week. How many deliveries did he complete in 7 weeks?

(A)   89   (B)   98   (C)   95   (D)   105

20   Lisa's parents are having a party. The family wanted to host the party in their backyard. They set up 9 tables, and each table can seat 8 people. How many people can be seated?

(A)   72   (B)   79   (C)   85   (D)   89

Next Section: Division Within 100 ➤➤

DIVISION WITHIN 100

Division within 100 refers to the ability to divide a number up to 100 into equal parts. Understanding division within 100 is an important skill for future math concepts, such as fractions, decimals, and algebra.

Example: $24 \div 2 = 12$ and $24 \div 12 = 2$

MULTIPLICATION AND DIVISION

1.3 Division Within 100

1 Oliver makes dinner for his sisters. He makes 50 sandwiches. If each of the sisters gets 5 sandwiches, how many sisters does Oliver have?

(A) 20   (B) 10   (C) 15   (D) 25

2 There are 96 cars in the parking garage. If there are the same number of cars on 6 floors, how many cars are parked on each floor?

(A) 16   (B) 18   (C) 22   (D) 25

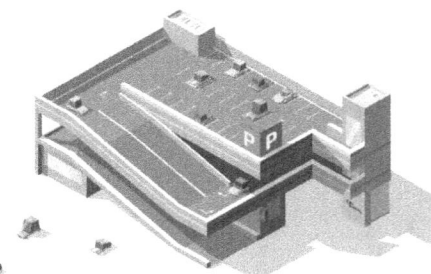

3 Eight friends were staying with James, and he planned to give donuts to his friends for breakfast. He prepared 48 donuts. If he shares the donuts equally, how many donuts does each friend get?

(A) 7   (B) 5   (C) 8   (D) 6

4 Ella planned to place books on her shelf and she has 72 books with her. If she has placed books equally on 4 shelves, how many books are there on each shelf?

(A) 19   (B) 18   (C) 12   (D) 15

5 Emily prepared 24 ice cream cones for her kids. How many ice creams will each of her three children get if they are shared equally?

(A) 8   (B) 4   (C) 6   (D) 7

6 Ava purchases 90 m rope and shares it equally with 5 of her friends, how much rope will each friend get?

(A) 16m   (B) 15m   (C) 14m   (D) 18m

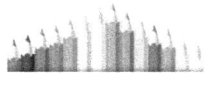

7 Mila is planning to organize her colored pencils into boxes. If she has 78 colored pencils and 6 boxes. How many pencils will be in each box?

(A) 15 color pencils   (B) 12 color pencils

(C) 13 color pencils   (D) 19 color pencils

8 Lucas has 11 white shirts and 55 black shirts. He places them in equal stacks on his shelf. He has 6 shelves. How many shirts are on each shelf?

(A) 7 shirts   (B) 8 shirts   (C) 10 shirts   (D) 11 shirts

MULTIPLICATION AND DIVISION

1.3 Division Within 100

09 Jacob is planning a birthday party. He spends $98 to purchase the balloons. Each balloon cost $7. How many balloons did he purchase?

- (A) 12
- (B) 14
- (C) 16
- (D) 18

10 In the school, there are 39 boys and 30 girls. If they are arranged in three equal groups how many people will be in each group?

- (A) 23
- (B) 25
- (C) 29
- (D) 21

11 Stella wants to give gifts to her family and friends for Halloween. She has $100 to spend and each gift costs $4. How many gifts will she be able to purchase?

- (A) $25
- (B) $21
- (C) $19
- (D) $29

12 Ivy makes paintings for her 8 classmates. How much time does she spend on each painting if she finishes them in 88 minutes?

- (A) 10 minutes
- (B) 11 minutes
- (C) 7 minutes
- (D) 8 minutes

13 Ellie has 36 flowers and 6 vases. She puts an equal number of flowers in each vase. How many flowers does Ellie put in each vase?

(A) 6   (B) 5   (C) 7   (D) 9

14 Ethan bought 35 Candies and 33 cookies. He shared equally with his 4 brothers. How many snacks will each brother get?

(A) 18   (B) 19   (C) 15   (D) 17

15 Students were divided into eight teams for a football game. If the class has 72 students, how many students will be on each team?

(A) 11   (B) 9   (C) 8   (D) 19

16 Ava makes 69 cheeseburgers for her birthday party. If she plans to give each person 3 cheeseburgers, how many people will get cheeseburgers?

(A) 21   (B) 23   (C) 29   (D) 25

MULTIPLICATION AND DIVISION

1.3   Division Within 100

17 Jack likes to bake. He baked pastries for friends during the holidays. He baked 84 pastries and put them on a table in 7 rows. How many pastries are in each row?

(A) 15   (B) 10   (C) 12   (D) 18

18 Luna spent $56 buying flowers at the florist. Each flower costs $8. How many flowers did Luna buy?

(A) $9   (B) $8   (C) $6   (D) $7

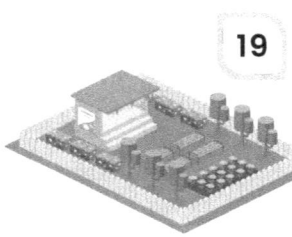

19 If a rectangular park area is 54 square meters and the width of the park is 6, calculate the length of the park. (Given: Area of a rectangular / length= width)

(A) 8 meters   (B) 9 meters   (C) 7 meters   (D) 3 meters

20 Hays reads each weekday. His book has 100 pages. If he reads 10 pages per day. How many days will it take to complete the book?

(A) 11   (C) 15

(B) 16   (D) 10

Next Section: Multiplication and Division Within 100 Involving Arrays and Measurements

MULTIPLICATION AND DIVISION WITHIN 100 INVOLVING ARRAYS AND MEASUREMENTS

This lesson is similar to the previous lesson in that it provides practice for multiplication and division within 100. Multiplication and division within 100 involving arrays and measurements refers to using arrays and measurements to solve problems related to multiplication and division.

The difference comes in where this lesson does arithmetic that involves measurement quantities. Students are exposed to real world word problems that involve equal groups and arrays with measurement quantities involved. In division, this means that the dividend and divisor are factors and leave no remainder when divided.

Example: 33 g ÷ 11 = 3 g and 33 g ÷ 3 = 11 g

3 × 11 g = 33 g and 11 g × 3 = 33 g

MULTIPLICATION AND DIVISION

1.4   **Multiplication and Division Within 100 Involving Arrays and Measurements**

1 Emma has invited 12 friends to her birthday party. She has 96 muffins. How many muffins will each friend get?

- (A) 5
- (B) 6
- (C) 8
- (D) 9

2 A rope is 48 cm long. The rope is cut into 6 equal pieces. What is the length of each 3 piece?

- (A) 24 cm
- (B) 12 cm
- (C) 16 cm
- (D) 36 cm

3 There were 80 foxes in the jungle. They usually hid in dens during the day. There were 10 dens in the jungle. If the foxes split themselves equally among the dens, how many foxes were there in each of the dens?

- (A) 90
- (B) 8
- (C) 80
- (D) 70

4 Liam ran 16 times around his playground during recess. If he ran a total of 96 m, how far is one loop around the playground?

- (A) 5m
- (B) 6m
- (C) 7m
- (D) 8m

5 If a carpenter uses 90 m wood to make 15 windows, how much wood would he use to make 4 windows?

(A) 32 m   (B) 10m   (C) 12m   (D) 24 m

6 Ethan has 21 baseball cards and 19 basketball cards. He wants to divide the cards into 4 equal boxes. Which value is the best estimate of how many cards he will put into each box?

(A) 5 cards   (B) 10 cards   (C) 15 cards   (D) 20 cards

7 James is going on a field trip with his classmates. 17 students can be seated on a school bus. If there are 3 buses, how many students are going on this trip?

(A) 51   (B) 61

(C) 49   (D) 20

8 For each lawn that Larry mows, he earns $8. How many lawns does he need to mow to buy a video game that costs $48?

(A) 9   (B) 8   (C) 6   (D) 7

MULTIPLICATION AND DIVISION

Multiplication and Division Within 100 Involving Arrays and Measurements

9 There were 23 crows and they laid 3 eggs each. How many eggs are there in all?

A) 59   B) 69   C) 91   D) 29

10 A wedding cake is made of 9 layers of equal height. The total height of the cake is 81 cm. What is the height of each layer of the cake?

A) 5   B) 6   C) 9   D) 8

11 The temperature on a spring day was 72 degrees in the morning. During the afternoon, the temperature rose 5 degrees, and then at night, it was 67 degrees. How much did the temperature drop from the afternoon to night?

A) 9 degrees   B) 10 degrees   C) 11 degrees   D) 12 degrees

12 There are 25 students in a classroom. There are 100 crayons. How many crayons will each students get?

A) 4   B) 5   C) 7   D) 8

13 A carpenter needs 8 m of wood to make a window pane. How much wood will he need to make 9 such window panes?

(A) 17 m (B) 18 m (C) 11 m (D) 72 m

14 Aiden saved $6 a day for 4 days. He wants to buy new sneakers that cost $30 dollars. How many more days does Aiden have to work so he will have enough money to buy the sneakers?

(A) 1 day (B) 2 days (C) 3 days (D) 4 days

15 Parker is having trouble solving $42 \div 7$. She can use the multiplication fact 7×5 and then:

(A) Add a group of 5 (B) Add a group of 7
(C) Subtract a group of 5 (D) Subtract a group of 7

16 The garden had 16 trees. The trees had an equal number of mangoes every day. If there were 80 mangoes, how many mangoes were there on each tree?

(A) 4 (B) 3 (C) 6 (D) 5

MULTIPLICATION AND DIVISION

1.4   **Multiplication and Division Within 100 Involving Arrays and Measurements**

17   Ava says any number that is divisible by 8 is also divisible by 4. Is she correct? Explain her reasoning.

_____

18   Explain how you can solve this equation using pictures, arrays, or a number line. $24 \div 4 = n$.

_____

19   Emily has $55 left over from her birthday party. Five days later, she had $5 left. If she spent the same amount of money on lunch every day, how much did she pay for lunch? Explain how you found your answer using an equation.

_____

20   Mia participated in a triathlon. Each leg of the race is a different event. She ran, cycled, and swam equal distances. If she covered a total of 78 m, what is the distance covered in each leg of the race?

_____

Next Section: Chapter Review ≫

1   Count the shapes and the number of groups and fill in the boxes.

_____

2   Helen delivers 11 milk boxes 5 times a week. How many milk boxes did he deliver in a week?

(A) 55 milk boxes   (B) 50 milk boxes

(C) 6 milk boxes   (D) 16 milk boxes

3   Use the picture to create a division number sentence.

_____ ÷ _____ = _____.

MULTIPLICATION AND DIVISION

4 Ryan has 28 keys, and he divides the keys into 7 equal groups. How many keys will there be in each group?

(A) 2 keys   (B) 3 keys   (C) 4 keys   (D) 5 keys

5 Use the arrays below and answer the following questions.

How many erasers are there in each row?

_____ ÷ _____ = _____.

6 78 mice were living in 13 nests. How many mice were in each nest if all the nests has an equal number of mice?

(A) 8 mice in each nest   (B) 6 mice in each nest

(C) 4 mice in each nest   (D) 65 mice in each nest

7 Which multiplication facts match this array?

(A) 3 × 4 and 4 × 3   (B) 4 × 5 and 5 × 4

(C) 2 × 6 and 6 × 2   (D) 3 × 2 and 2 × 3

8 Mia has 24 flowers and 4 vases. She puts an equal number of flowers in each vase. How many flowers does Mia put in each vase?

(A) 28   (B) 4   (C) 22   (D) 6

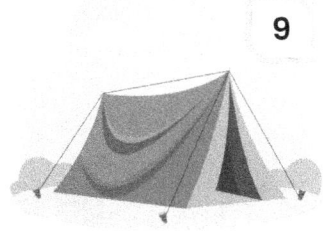

9 Fifteen girls scouts are going camping. Each tent sleeps 3 people. How many tents should the girl scouts bring so everyone has a place to sleep?

(A) 5 tents   (B) 8 tents   (C) 3 tents   (D) 6 tents

10 For weekend homework, Max had 18 multiplication problems and 24 division problems. Max can do 7 math problems in an hour. How many hours will it take him to solve the problem?

(A) 4 hours   (B) 7 hours

(C) 5 hours   (D) 6 hours

1.5   **Chapter Review**

11 A phone takes two hours to charge from 0 to 100%. Emily's family members take turns charging of their phones one after the other. They take 20 hours to charge all their phones. How many phones does Emily's family have?

(A) 6 phones   (B) 8 phones   (C) 10 phones   (D) 20 phones

12 Which equation can be used to determine the total number of apples in this picture?

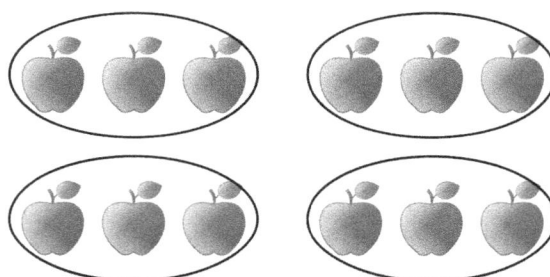

(A) 3 + 3 + 3 + 3 =

(B) 4 + 4 + 4 =

(C) 3 + 4 + 3 =

(D) 4 + 4 + 3 =

13 Roshan works 10 hours a week. He earns $ 9 each hour. How much money does Roshan earn in a week?

(A) $ 75   (B) $ 70   (C) $ 18   (D) $ 90

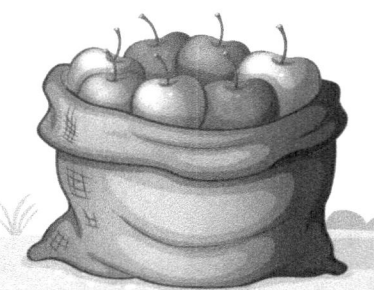

14   Noah bought 3 bags with 7 red apples in each bag and 4 bags with 6 green apples in each bag. How many apples did Noah buy altogether?

(A) 42 apples   (B) 45 apples   (C) 52 apples   (D) 48 apples

15   Parker bought 30 Guavas. He gave 6 guavas to each of her friends. How many friends does Parker have?

(A) 3 friends   (B) 2 friends

(C) 4 friends   (D) 5 friends

16   Mary decides to make bracelets to give to her friends. She has 36 pieces of blue string, 4 pieces of yellow string, and 30 pieces of red string. She uses 10 strings for each bracelet.
How many friends will receive a bracelet?

(A) 70   (B) 8   (C) 7   (D) 60

17   Travis is organizing his video game collection. He has 63 video games to organize on 7 shelves. He thinks of this as a division problem $63 \div 7 = n$. What other equation can be used to determine the number of video games Travis will put on each shelf?

(A) $n = 63 \times 7$ (B) $63 - 7 = n$ (C) $63 = n \times 7$ (D) $7 + n = 6$

1.5   Chapter Review

18 Mr. Peter needs 64 cups for his party. The cups come in packs of 8. How many packs should Mr. Peter buy for the party?

(A) 7   (B) 8   (C) 9   (D) 6

19 There are 12 windows in every house in a neighborhood. Max is the painter who is asked to paint all the windows red. If he paints 84 windows, how many houses are there in the neighborhood?

(A) 6   (B) 4   (C) 3   (D) 7

20 There were 52 passengers waiting for their taxis at the airport. 13 cars drove in to pick up the waiting passengers. If the cars had an equal number of passengers, how many were there in each car?

(A) 3   (B) 4   (C) 5   (D) 7

Next Chapter: Relationship Between Multiplication and Division

CHAPTER 2

RELATIONSHIP BETWEEN MULTIPLICATION AND DIVISION

COMPLETE THE PATTERN

PROPERTIES OF MULTIPLICATION

The properties of multiplication are rules that describe how multiplication works. Two main properties of multiplication: the commutative property and the distributive property.

Commutative Property: This property states that the order of the factors does not change the product.

For example: $5 \times 6 = 6 \times 5$.

 $5 \times 6 = 30$

 $6 \times 5 = 30$

Distributive Property: This property states that we can break up a factor into smaller parts and distribute the multiplication over each part.

For example: $5 \times (4 + 2) = (5 \times 4) + (5 \times 2)$.

$5 \times (4 + 2)$

$(5 \times 4) + (5 \times 2)$

PROPERTIES OF MULTIPLICATION

Another property of multiplication that students may encounter is the associative property. This property states that the grouping of the factors does not change the product.

For example: $(3 \times 4) \times 5 = 3 \times (4 \times 5)$.

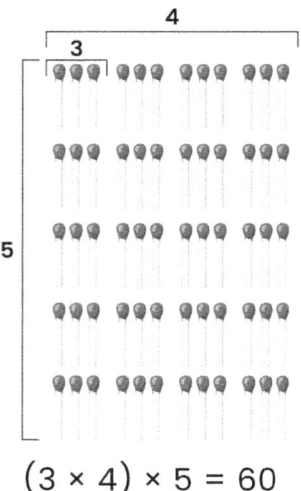

$(3 \times 4) \times 5 = 60$

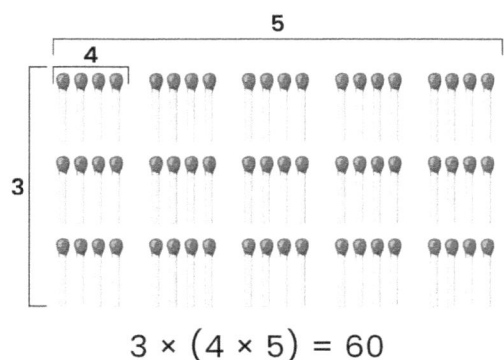

$3 \times (4 \times 5) = 60$

1 Which property is modeled in this equation? $4 \times (3 \times 8) = (4 \times 3) \times 8$

(A) Commutative Property of Multiplication

(B) Associative Property of Multiplication

(C) Distributive Property

(D) None of the above

2 Complete the statement using distributive property.

$4 \times (3+7) = ($ _____ $\times$ _____ $) + ($ _____ $\times$ _____ $)$

3 Farmer Andrew has a garden with two sections of plants. Each section has 5 rows of 11 plants. How many plants does farmer Andrew have planted in each section of his garden? Write two commutative multiplication sentences and calculate how many plants farmer Andrew has planted in each section of his garden.

_____

4 Which equation shows the distributive property?

(A) $5 + 3 = 8$ (B) $2 \times 4 = 4 \times 2$

(C) $3(2+3) = (3 \times 2) + (3 \times 3)$ (D) $5 \times 3 = 15$

RELATIONSHIP BETWEEN MULTIPLICATION AND DIVISION

2.1 Properties of Multiplication

5 Which equation shows the commutative property of multiplication?

(A) $8 \times 2 = 16$

(B) $5(3 + 1) = 15 + 5$

(C) $8 + 2 = 2 + 8$

(D) $4 \times 8 = 8 \times 4$

6 Silvia arranged eight rows of chairs for her birthday party. Each row has 7 chairs. Jessy also arranged eight rows of 7 chairs. Write two associative multiplication sentences and calculate how many chairs they arranged in all.

(A) 112 chairs　(B) 42 chairs　(C) 49 chairs　(D) 63 chairs

7 Draw two arrays to represent this expression: $5(2 + 8)$

_____

8 Complete the blank using the commutative property.
$8 \times 5 = 5 \times$ _____.

(A) 4　(B) 7　(C) 8　(D) 6

9 If 12 times the sum of 6 and another number is 132, find the other number.

(A) 4　(B) 5　(C) 6　(D) 7

Properties of Multiplication   **2.1**

10 Write the multiplication sentences and find the answers for each commutative picture block.

_____ X _____ = _____ .   _____ X _____ = _____ .

11 Complete the statement using the associative property.

$9 \times (3 \times 5) = (9 \times$ _____ $) \times$ _____ .

12 The expression $6 \times (7+2)$ is the same as:

   Ⓐ $(6 \times 7) + (6 \times 2)$ Ⓑ $(6 + 7) + (6 + 2)$

   Ⓒ $(6 + 7) \times (6 + 2)$ Ⓓ $(6 \times 7) \times (6 \times 2)$

13 Maria purchases an equal number of broccoli and cabbages. Each broccoli costs $5, and each cabbage costs $4. She spends a total of $108 at the vegetable shop. How many broccoli and cabbages did she buy in all?

   Ⓐ 13   Ⓑ 14   Ⓒ 12   Ⓓ 10

2.1 Properties of Multiplication

14 Mercy is preparing cupcakes for her friend's birthday party. She uses 8 chocolate chips on each cupcake. She prepares 18 cupcakes. Use distributive law to calculate the number of chocolate chips Mercy uses in her cupcakes.

A) 132　　　B) 128　　　C) 153　　　D) 144

15 Simplify: $7 \times (c+d)$

A) $(7+c) \times d$　　B) $(7+d) \times c$　　C) $(7 \times c) + (7 \times d)$　　D) $(7+c)$

16 Write the multiplication sentences and find the answers for each commutative picture block.

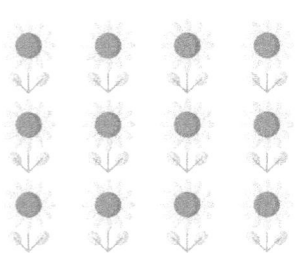
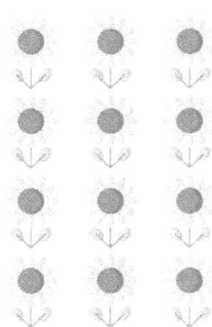

_____ × _____ = _____ .　　_____ × _____ = _____ .

17 Which equation shows the commutative property of multiplication?

A) $7 \times 3 = 2 \times 7$　　B) $43 + 2 = 12 + 8$

C) $7 + 2 = 2 + 7$　　D) $9 \times 5 = 5 \times 9$

Properties of Multiplication 2.1

18 Complete the statement using the associative property.

$8 \times (2 \times 7) = (8 \times$ _____ $) \times$ _____.

19 State "True" or "False".
Commutative property: $3 \times 9 = 9 \times 3$

(A) True   (B) False

20 Which of the multiplication sentences is distributive? Which of the multiplication sentences is distributive?

(A) $3 \times (6+11) = (3\times6) + (3\times10)$ (B) $1 \times (8+9) = (1\times9) + (1\times7)$

(C) $2 \times (7+10) = (2\times7) + (2\times9)$ (D) $5 \times (4+9) = (5\times4) + (5\times9)$

Next Section: Relation Between Multiplication and Division

RELATION BETWEEN MULTIPLICATION AND DIVISION

The relation between multiplication and division is that they are inverse operations, which means that they undo each other.

Students get to understand the relationship between multiplication and division, enabling them to use either of the operations to solve real-life problems.

Example:
12 × 4 = 48 can also be written as 48 ÷ 4 = 12.

1 David needs 72 plates for his party. The plates come in a pack of 9. How many packs should David buy for the party?

(A) 9   (B) 8   (C) 10   (D) 7

2 A train with 8 passenger cars is 80 m long. Each passenger car has an equal length. What is the length of the train with 6 passenger cars?

_____

3 Which model represents this equation? $15 \div 3 = 5$

(A)

(B)

(C)

(D)

4 Jack is sorting through his video games. He has 64 video games to organize on 8 shelves. He thinks of this as a division problem $64 \div 8 = n$. What other equation can be used to solve this problem?

(A) $n = 64 \times 8$ (B) $64 - 8 = n$ (C) $64 = n \times 8$ (D) $8 + n = 64$

2.2   Relation Between Multiplication and Division

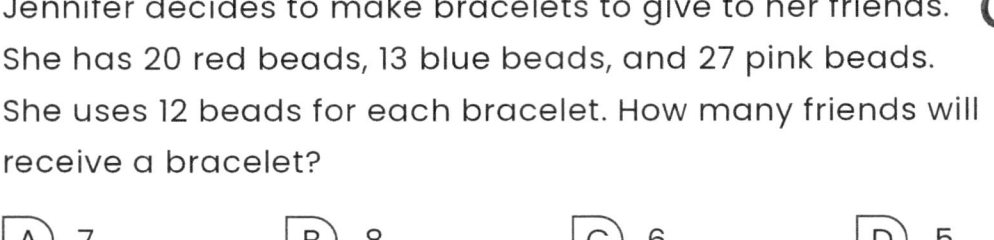

5   Jennifer decides to make bracelets to give to her friends. She has 20 red beads, 13 blue beads, and 27 pink beads. She uses 12 beads for each bracelet. How many friends will receive a bracelet?

Ⓐ 7   Ⓑ 8   Ⓒ 6   Ⓓ 5

6   A rope is 120 m long. It is cut into 15 pieces of equal length. Each piece is used to make squares with equal sides. What is the length of each side?

_____

7   The distance between Andrea's house and the swimming pool is 7 km. If she goes to the pool 5 days a week for practice, what is the total distance traveled?

Ⓐ 70 km   Ⓑ 38 km   Ⓒ 42 km   Ⓓ 45 km

8   If 4 people in a relay race cover a distance of 120 m, what is the distance covered by each of them?

_____

9 If an apple weighs 180 g. How much do 5 apples weigh?

(A) 900 g   (B) 750 g   (C) 1000 g   (D) 550 g

10 Jenny has 13 jugs of mango juice, each of which has a capacity of 2 liters. How much juice did Jenny have in all?

_____

11 For a birthday party, they ordered a cake with 6 layers of equal height. The total height of the cake is 96 cm. What is the height of each layer of the cake?

(A) 15 cm   (B) 16 cm   (C) 12 cm   (D) 13 cm

12 7 hexagons were created using an 84 cm long rope. What is the length of each side of the hexagon?

_____

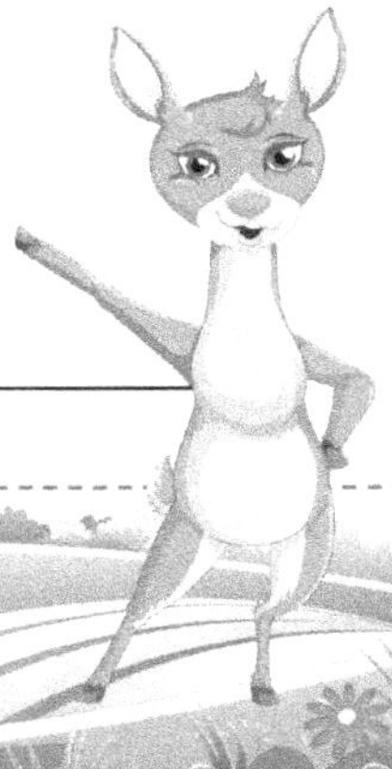

2.2 **Relation Between Multiplication and Division**

13 If the length of 6 drawing books is 54 cm, what is the length of 11 books?

(A) 72 cm   (B) 99 cm   (C) 63 cm   (D) 86 cm

14 Jessy has 5 bags with 7 colored boxes in each bag. She gives away 10 colored boxes and receives 5 more from her friend. Which equation represents the number of books Jessy has left?

(A) $(5 \times 7) - (10 - 5) = n$ (B) $(5 + 7) - (10 + 5) = n$

(C) $(5 \times 7) - 10 + 5 = n$ (D) $(5 \times 7) + (10 - 5) = n$

15 Peter is trying to simplify this expression: 7×5.
Which expression is equivalent to 7×5?

(A) $(7 \times 3) + (7 \times 2)$ (B) $(7 \times 4) + (7 \times 5)$

(C) $(7 \times 3) + (7 \times 4)$ (D) $(7 \times 3) - (7 \times 5)$

16 Martin spent his allowance of $72 buying oranges from the fruit shop. Each orange cost $8. Which equation represents the number of oranges Martin bought?

(A) $72 - 8 = 64$ (B) $72 \div 8 = 9$

(C) $9 \times 8 = 72$ (D) $72 \div 8 = 7$

17 Steffi is having trouble simplifying the expression 7×7. Which strategy can she use?

(A) 7×5 and then add one group of 9

(B) 7×6 and then add one group of 8

(C) 7×8 and subtract one group of 7

(D) 7×9 and subtract one group of 9

18 Holly wanted to buy balloons for all her students. Each balloon costs \$2. If she spent money \$70 to buy the balloons, how many balloons did she get?

(A) 29   (B) 38   (C) 42   (D) 35

19 Pizza House customers are encouraged to ring the bell twice if they had a good experience at the restaurant. On a given day, the bell rings 52 times. How many customers enjoyed eating there?

(A) 26   (B) 38   (C) 23   (D) 35

20 The height of 15 bricks is 90 cm. What is the height of 8 bricks arranged one over the other?

Next Section: Chapter Review »

RELATIONSHIP BETWEEN MULTIPLICATION AND DIVISION

Chapter Review

1 A school uniform costs $10 jerseys and $7 shorts. How much will 6 sets of uniforms cost?

(A) 102 (B) 98 (C) 89 (D) 92

2 If an orange weighs 120 g. How much does do 7 such oranges weigh?

(A) 905 g (B) 840 g (C) 1010 g (D) 520 g

3 Complete the equation using the associative property.
$7 \times (6 \times 8) = (7 \times \underline{\qquad}) \times \underline{\qquad}.$

4 Which model represents this equation? $20 \div 4 = 5$

(A)
(B)
(C)
(D)

5 Sam went to a fruit shop. There were 9 baskets, and each basket had 5 fruits in it. How much fruit was in the shop?

(A) 42 (B) 58 (C) 45 (D) 52

6 Write associative statements using the numbers 4, 7 and 13.

(A) $13 \times (2 + 3)$

(B) $4 \times (7 + 5)$

(C) $(4 \times 13) + (7 \times 13)$

(D) $4 \times (7 \times 13) = (4 \times 7) \times 13$

7 Elisa needs 63 cups for the function. The cups come in a pack of 7. How many packs should Elisa buy for the function?

(A) 8

(B) 9

(C) 10

(D) 7

8 Complete the statement using the distributive property.
$7 \times (2+6) = ($ _____ $\times$ _____ $) + ($ _____ $\times$ _____ $)$

9 The distance between Lisa's house and the tennis court is 5 km. If she goes to tennis practice 6 days a week, what is the total distance traveled?

(A) 60 km

(B) 38 km

(C) 42 km

(D) 45 km

10 Anthony gets 42 new bike toys. If the bike toys come in packs of 6, how many packs of bike toys did Anthony get?

(A) 9

(B) 8

(C) 7

(D) 10

2.3   Chapter Review

11 Write the multiplication sentences and find the answers for each commutative picture block.

_____ x _____ = _____

_____ x _____ = _____

12 A 100 cm long rope was used to make 5 pentagons. What is the length of each side of the pentagon?

Ⓐ 5 cm   Ⓑ 4 cm   Ⓒ 6 cm   Ⓓ 7 cm

13 Blessy arranged 7 chocolate boxes for the Christmas party. Each box has 6 chocolates. Angel also did the same. How many chocolates are there altogether?

Ⓐ 84   Ⓑ 95   Ⓒ 86   Ⓓ 72

14 Lucas makes an array using 4 rows of 7 stickers. How many stickers does Lucas have if he adds 3 more rows to the array?

Ⓐ 45   Ⓑ 39   Ⓒ 42   Ⓓ 49

15   Which equation shows the distributive property?

(A) $4 + 7 = 11$ (B) $3 \times 4 = 4 \times 3$

(C) $2(3 + 4) = (2 \times 3) + (2 \times 4)$ (D) $5 \times 4 = 20$

16   Angelina uses a number line to count by 7 to reach 63. If she starts at zero, how many times did Angelina count by 7 to reach 63?

(A) 9   (B) 14   (C) 10   (D) 12

17   Which equation shows the commutative property of multiplication?

(A) $8 \times 2 = 16$ (B) $5(3+1) = 15 + 5$

(C) $8 + 2 = 2 + 8$ (D) $7 \times 6 = 6 \times 7$

18   The children are playing with the building blocks. The height of 12 blocks is 96 cm. What is the height of 6 blocks arranged one over the other?

2.3 **Chapter Review**

19 Angel buys an equal number of strawberries and kiwis. Each strawberry costs $4, and each kiwi costs $6. She spends a total of $90 at the fruit shop. How many strawberries and kiwis did she buy in all?

(A) 13   (B) 14   (C) 10   (D) 12

20 A carpenter uses 60 m of wood to make 12 windows. How much wood would he use to make 8 windows?

Next Chapter: Place Value >>

CHAPTER 3

PLACE VALUE

COMPLETE THE PATTERN

 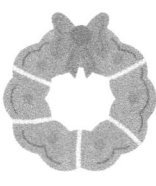  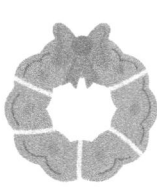 

ROUND WHOLE NUMBERS TO THE NEAREST 10 OR 100

Rounding is a math concept that involves changing a number to a nearby value that is easier to work with or understand

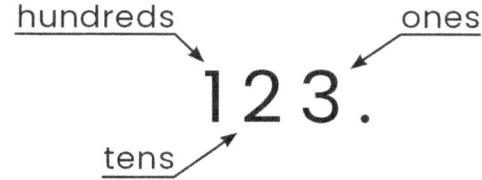

To round a whole number to the nearest 10, look at the ones digit of the number. If the ones digit is 0 to 4, they round down to the nearest 10. If the ones digit is 5 to 9, they round up to the nearest 10

To round a whole number to the nearest 100, look at the last two digits of the number. If the last two digits are 00 to 49, they round down to the nearest 100. If the last two digits are 50 to 99, they round up to the nearest 100.

Example:

The number 637 has 6 hundreds (or 600), 3 tens (or 30) and 7 ones (or 7).

If we are given 6 hundreds, 3 tens, and 7 ones, we can put them together to get the number 637 = 600 + 30 + 7.

Round 637 to the nearest hundred.

First, we identify the value in the hundreds place: 6

Then, we identify the value in the place value immediately to the right, in this case the tens place: 3

Since 3<5 , we leave the value in the hundreds place alone and replace the rest of the values with 0.

Therefore, 637 rounded to the nearest hundred is 600.

PLACE VALUE

3.1   **Round Whole Numbers to The Nearest 10 or 100**

1 What place value is represented by the underlined value?

9̲99

(A) Ones   (B) Tens   (C) Hundreds   (D) Units

2 Write the number that corresponds with the number of ones, tens, and hundreds.

7 hundreds, 5 tens, 3 ones.

(A) 357   (B) 753   (C) 573   (D) 777

3 Round to the nearest ten - 867.

(A) 870   (B) 860   (C) 800   (D) 900

4 Round to the nearest hundred - 139.

(A) 500   (B) 400   (C) 300   (D) 100

5 Select the answer by rounding up or down to the nearest hundred.

891 - 348 = ?

(A) 900   (B) 600   (C) 400   (D) 800

6   Select the answer by rounding up or down to the nearest hundred.

567 + 648 = ?

(A) 1200   (B) 1000   (C) 1100   (D) 900

7   Rebecca made apple juice using 155 apples. Which number represents the number of apples used, rounded to the nearest 10?

(A) 140   (B) 150   (C) 160   (D) 170

8   Micah planted 309 rose plants in her garden. Which number represents the number of rose plants she planted, rounded to the nearest 100?

(A) 410   (B) 400   (C) 310   (D) 300

9   Ari harvests between 700 and 800 carrots. The number of carrots rounded to the nearest hundred is closer to 800. Which number could represent the actual number of carrots?

(A) 657   (B) 783   (C) 673   (D) 717

PLACE VALUE

3.1   Round Whole Numbers to The Nearest 10 or 100

10 An orange tree produces between 500 and 600 oranges. The number of oranges, rounded to the nearest ten is 500. Which number could represent the actual number of oranges?

(A) 417   (B) 553   (C) 510   (D) 707

11 Brenden is collecting stamps. He already has 62, and adds 19 to his collection. Which number shows the number of stamps he has rounded to the nearest ten?

(A) 80   (B) 70   (C) 60   (D) 20

12 Greta has 23 pens. Which number represents Greta's total number of pens, rounded to the nearest 100?

(A) 30   (B) 20   (C) 1   (D) 0

13 The shop has 175 donuts. Which number represents the number of donuts the shop has rounded to the nearest 10?

(A) 170   (B) 180   (C) 190   (D) 200

14 The cake shop contains nearly 300 cakes. The estimate is found by rounding the actual number to the nearest 10. Which number represents the actual number of cakes in the cake shop?

(A) 298   (B) 359   (C) 387   (D) 256

15 The vegetable shop has close to 2,000 vegetables. This estimate is found by rounding the actual number to the nearest 100. Which number represents the actual number of vegetables in the vegetable shop?

(A) 1101   (B) 1901   (C) 2101   (D) 2999

16 Dixie made 1,915 candles. How many candles does she made rounded to the nearest 100?

(A) 1800   (B) 2000   (C) 1500   (D) 1900

17 Drake collects teddy bears and has 444 teddy bears. Rounded to the nearest ten, about how many teddy bears does Drake have?

3.1   **Round Whole Numbers to The Nearest 10 or 100**

18   You collect stickers and have 4,969 bird stickers. Rounded to the nearest hundred, about how many bird stickers do you have?

_____

19   Kyle has 15 fewer notebooks than Levi. Levi rounds the number of notebooks he has to the nearest ten and has about 50 notebooks. Which number could represent the number of notebooks Kyle has?

_____

20   While driving, you see 432 bikes. Rounded to the nearest ten, about how many bikes did you see?

_____

Next Section: Add and Subtract Within 1000 ≫

ADD AND SUBTRACT WITHIN 1000

Add numbers within 1000 means they will be able to add numbers with up to three digits

Example: Add 243+456 using place value splitting.

First, we break each number down by place value:

$$243 = 200 + 40 + 3$$
$$456 = 400 + 50 + 6$$

Then, we sum the place values:

$$200+400=600$$
$$40+50=90$$
$$3+6=9$$

Finally, we reconstruct the number:

$$600+90+9=699$$

The shortcut approach for subtraction: In addition, we borrow from one of the addends so that we are adding friendly numbers (a number that is a multiple of ten). In subtraction, we add the same value to both numbers to make the larger number a friendly number (a number that has a 9 in the ones place).

Example:

Subtract 456 - 243 using the shortcut approach.

We want the larger value to have a 9 in the ones place. To accomplish this, we need to add 3 to each value.

$$456 + 3 - 243 + 3 = 459 - 246$$

This gives us an "easy" number from which to subtract, and we complete the subtraction.

3.2   **Add and Subtract Within 1000**

1 Which number makes this equation true?

521 + 326 - 287 = _____ + 208

(A) 398   (B) 352   (C) 387   (D) 356

2  Miller buys a box of ice cream. There are 150 pieces inside the box. He gives 40 pieces to each of his friends and eats 20 pieces. Which number sentence can be used to determine how many ice creams he has left?

(A) 150 − (40-40) − 20   (B) 150 + (40+40) + 20

(C) 150 − (40-40) + 20   (D) 150 − (40+40) − 20

3 Which number makes this equation true?

790 - 206 + 187 = 909 - _____.

4 878 - 357 = _____.

(A) 521   (B) 652   (C) 587   (D) 656

Add and Subtract Within 1000   3.2

5 The school cafeteria has 182 students seated. The school cafeteria can serve 295 students. How many seats are empty?

(A) 154   (B) 181

(C) 113   (D) 198

6 Tegan bought 111 lemons in February. In February and January combined, she bought 354 lemons. How many lemons did she buy in January?

(A) 301   (B) 324   (C) 231   (D) 243

7 Stanley takes 216 minutes to complete an exercise 1 in math. He takes 278 minutes to complete exercise 2. How much time did he take to complete both exercises?

_____

8 Paul walked for 399 hours last year. He walked for 428 hours this year. How many hours has he spent walking, combined?

(A) 399   (B) 827   (C) 428   (D) 872

3.2 **Add and Subtract Within 1000**

9 A farmer has 875 watermelons. He sold 451 watermelons. How many watermelons are left?

_____

10 Roy earned $381 this month. After spending $150 on new items, how much money does he have left?

_____

11 Wesley has 178 chocolates. His sister has 215 chocolates. How many chocolates do they have combined?

(A) 199   (B) 227   (C) 393   (D) 472

12 The store has 289 door curtains and 587 window curtains. How many curtains do they have in total?

(A) 876   (B) 847   (C) 813   (D) 872

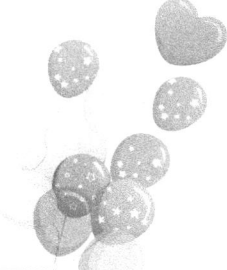

13 The room contains 897 balloons, with 298 of them being green. How many balloons in the room are pink?

_____

14 A garden contains 558 rose plants. 252 rose plants have been sold. How many rose plants are left?

(A) 876   (B) 847   (C) 813   (D) 872

15 A storybook consists of 256 paragraphs. Randy read the storybook two times. How many paragraphs did he read in total?

(A) 512   (B) 256   (C) 501   (D) 289

16 Grade 3 students are going on a picnic 466 miles away. They have already driven 214 miles. How many miles do they have left to drive?

(A) 466   (B) 252   (C) 214   (D) 198

3.2   **Add and Subtract Within 1000**

17 Roy caught 778 fish. 352 fish are quite large. How many fish are small?

_____

18 625 + 359 = 984 can be rewritten as

984 - _____ = 359

(A) 615   (B) 984   (C) 625   (D) 359

19 Thomas bought a bicycle for $175. His brother bought a bicycle for $197. How much money is spent on both bicycles?

_____

20 Pierre saved $824. He spent $568 on his birthday party. How much money is left in his savings account?

(A) 387   (B) 296   (C) 345   (D) 256

Next Section: Multiply One-Digit Whole Numbers By Multiples of 10

MULTIPLY ONE-DIGIT WHOLE NUMBERS BY MULTIPLES OF 10

Multiply one-digit whole numbers by multiples of 10 means they will be able to find the product of a number with only one digit (0-9) and another number that is a multiple of 10

For example, 123 consists of 1 hundred, 2 tens, and 3 ones.

We can use this approach to understand multiplication by multiples of 10.

We'll start with a simple multiplication and slowly increase the complexity.

We know $3 \times 4 = 12$.

If we increase the complexity and change our problem to 3×4 tens, we get 12 tens. We know that 12 tens are the same as 120.

Therefore, we know $3 \times 40 = 120$.

Example:

Multiply 7×30 using multiplication facts and place value.

$7 \times 30 = 7 \times 3$ tens $= 21$ tens $= 210$.

Multiply One-Digit Whole Numbers
By Multiples of 10

3.3

1 What is the value of 5 tens?

(A) 50   (B) 30   (C) 40   (D) 15

2 Seth says he has six $10 bills. How much money does Seth have?

(A) 10   (B) 40   (C) 60   (D) 90

3 Tess has 4 boxes with 10 candies in each box. Which equation can be used to determine the total number of candies Tess has?

(A) 4 − 10 =   (B) 4 × 10 =   (C) 4 + 10 =   (D) 4 ÷ 10 =

4 A school bus can carry 60 students. How many students can 3 buses carry?

_____

5 Calvin has 70 pencils that he wants to share with 7 friends. Which equation can you use to determine how many pencils each friend receives?

_____

3.3 **Multiply One-Digit Whole Numbers By Multiples of 10**

6 Kai has 8 ten-dollar T-shirts, Loraine has 9 ten-dollar T-shirts, and Madeline has 2 ten-dollar T-shirts. In total, how much money are the T-shirts worth?

(A) $190   (B) $180   (C) $120   (D) $100

7 John needs paper cups for his birthday party. He buys 11 packs of 40 cups. How many cups did John buy?

(A) 410 cups   (B) 420 cups   (C) 430 cups   (D) 440 cups

8 Elliot earned a certain amount of money and now has thirteen $10 bills. How much money did Elliot earn?

_____

9 The fruit shop sells strawberries in packs of 80. Rose buys 7 packs of strawberries. Which equation can be used to find the total number of strawberries Rose bought?

(A) $1 \times 3 \times 5 = $ _____   (B) $7 \times 8 \times 10 = $ _____

(C) $7 + 8 + 10 = $ _____   (D) $1 + 3 + 5 = $ _____

10 If there are 60 minutes in one hour, how many minutes are in 12 hours and 10 minutes?

(A) 120 minutes (B) 600 minutes (C) 730 minutes (D) 100 minutes

11 Write the multiplication problem numerically
$$7 \times 5 \text{ tens}$$

(A) 7×5 (B) 7×50 (C) 7×500 (D) None of them

12 Solve the multiplication problem. $9 \times 10 =$ _____.

13 Hailey bought 5 boxes of pears. Each box contains 30 pears. How many pears did he buy?

(A) 110 (B) 130 (C) 150 (D) 180

14 Max drives 40 kilometers. If he does this 3 times a day, how many kilometers does he complete in total in a day?

(A) 120 (B) 230 (C) 350 (D) 460

3.3 Multiply One-Digit Whole Numbers
By Multiples of 10

15 If an 1 hour has 60 minutes, Tom has been working for 5 hours. How many minutes has he been working?

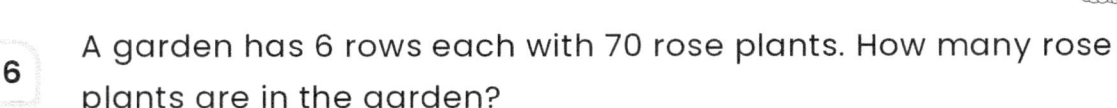

(A) 100 minutes   (B) 150 minutes

(C) 250 minutes   (D) 500 minutes

16 A garden has 6 rows each with 70 rose plants. How many rose plants are in the garden?

(A) 600   (B) 720   (C) 400   (D) 420

17 A ribbon length is 50 cm. Jerry has 5 ribbons. How much length do all the ribbons have?

(A) 100   (B) 150   (C) 250   (D) 500

18 There are 40 potatoes in a bag. How many potatoes are in the 4 bags?

19 A basket contains 80 balls. If Jaxon owns three basket, how many balls does he have?

_____

20 A pack contains 20 water bottles. If Zoe bought 4 packs of water bottles. How many water bottles does Zoe buy?

(A) 40   (B) 80   (C) 120   (D) 160

Next Section: Chapter Review »

3.4   **Chapter Review**

1 The car shop has 188 red cars, and 312 black cars. What is the total number of cars, rounded to the nearest hundred?

(A) 700   (B) 200   (C) 300   (D) 500

2 Enzo has 73 watches. Her brother buys 27 more. How many watches does he have, rounded to the nearest ten?

(A) 100   (B) 80   (C) 50   (D) 30

3 Gary gained $378 last month in his book shop. This month, he gained $514. Rounded to the nearest hundred, how much money did he gain?

_____

4 Sawyer has 2,524 sheep on his farm. Trice has 4,666 sheep on his farm. Rounded to the nearest hundred, about how many sheep do they have in all?

(A) 2600   (B) 7200   (C) 5000   (D) 4700

5 Toby drove for 63 hours this month. He drove for 36 hours last month, rounded to the nearest ten. About how many hours did he drive?

(A) 100   (B) 90   (C) 60   (D) 40

6 There are 496 students in an amusement park. There are 438 students at the zoo. Rounded to the nearest hundred, how many students are in the amusement park and zoo?

_____

7 Nicole collects stamps. She has 765 stamps currently. She received 298 more from her brother. Rounded to the nearest hundred, about how many stamps are in her collection now?

(A) 700   (B) 800   (C) 300   (D) 1100

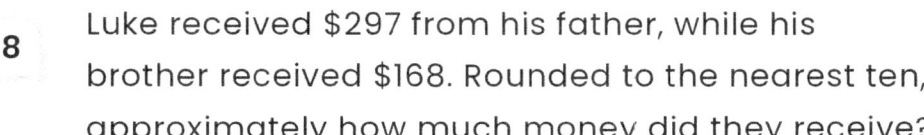

8 Luke received $297 from his father, while his brother received $168. Rounded to the nearest ten, approximately how much money did they receive?

(A) 290   (B) 470   (C) 170   (D) 430

3.4   **Chapter Review**

9   Ian received 178 gifts for his wedding. Rounded to the nearest ten, about how many gifts did he receive?

_____

10   Seamus saved $369. His mother gives him $175, which he spends $216 for a new bicycle. How much money does he have left?

(A) 309   (B) 312   (C) 328   (D) 376

11   What place value is represented by the underlined value?

765

(A) Ones   (B) Tens   (C) Hundreds

12   Write the number that corresponds with the number of ones, tens, and hundreds.

1 hundreds, 7 ones

(A) 17   (B) 701   (C) 107   (D) 170

13 You collect stickers and have 2,267 fruit stickers. Rounded to the nearest hundred, about how many fruit stickers do you have?

_____

14 Sean made 3,278 cupcakes. How many cupcakes does he make, rounded to the nearest 100?

A) 3270   B) 3200   C) 3280   D) 3300

15 Which number makes this equation true?
391 + 276 - 257 = _____ + 178

A) 398   B) 232   C) 387   D) 356

16 A pet shop has 682 dogs and cats. The shop has 411 dogs. How many cats are in a pet shop?

_____

PLACE VALUE

3.4   **Chapter Review**

17 What is the value of 1 tens?

(A) 10   (B) 100   (C) 110   (D) 111

18 Penelope has 6 boxes with 10 spoons in each box. Which equation can be used to determine the total number of spoons Penelope has?

(A) 6 – 10 =   (B) 6 ÷ 10 =   (C) 6 + 10 =   (D) 6 × 10 =

19 The vegetable shop sells tomatoes in packs of 70.
Jasmine buys 4 packs of tomatoes. Which equation can be used to find the total number of tomatoes Jasmine bought?

(A) 4×3×5=   (B) 4+7+10=   (C) 4×7×10=   (D) 4+3+5=

20 Write the multiplication problem numerically
$$3×1 \text{ tens}$$

(A) 3×1   (B) 3×10   (C) 3×100   (D) None of them

Next Chapter: Fractions ≫

CHAPTER 4

FRACTIONS

WHAT NEXT COMES?

COMPLETE THE PATTERN

DIVIDING "A" WHOLE INTO "B" PARTS AND A/B FRACTIONS

A fraction is a way to represent a part of a whole. To do this, the whole must be divided into equal parts.

A fraction consists of two parts: a numerator and a denominator.

The numerator is the top number in the fraction and is the number of pieces we have.

The denominator is the bottom number in the fraction and is the number of equal pieces that the whole was divided into.

$$\frac{\text{numerator}}{\text{denominator}}$$

The fraction $\frac{1}{2}$ has 1 as the numerator and 2 as the denominator. This means that the whole was divided into 2 equal parts and we have 1 of them. This is shown by the shaded part of the table below

We can write fractions in different ways. For example, instead of dividing the whole into 2 pieces, we can divide it into 4 pieces. Then, if we have 2 pieces of the 4 equal parts, we still have half of the pieces as shown in the table below.

We can carry this relationship on for quite a while. The table below shows the relationship between fractions.

1							
$\frac{1}{2}$				$\frac{1}{2}$			
$\frac{1}{4}$		$\frac{1}{4}$		$\frac{1}{4}$		$\frac{1}{4}$	
$\frac{1}{8}$	$\frac{1}{8}$	$\frac{1}{8}$	$\frac{1}{8}$	$\frac{1}{8}$	$\frac{1}{8}$	$\frac{1}{8}$	$\frac{1}{8}$

4.1 Dividing "A" Whole Into "B" Parts
and A/B Fractions

---

1 What is the denominator of the fraction? $\frac{1}{4}$

(A) 1   (B) 2   (C) 3   (D) 4

---

2 What is the numerator of the fraction? $\frac{2}{3}$

(A) 1   (B) 2   (C) 3   (D) 4

---

3 What fraction of the squares are shaded?

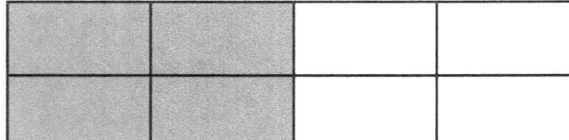

(A) $\frac{1}{4}$ (B) $\frac{2}{8}$

(C) $\frac{4}{8}$ (D) $\frac{3}{8}$

---

4 What fraction of the squares are shaded?

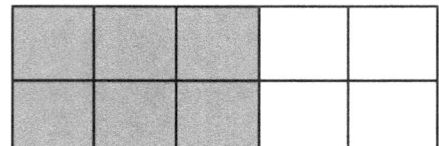

(A) $\frac{6}{8}$ (B) $\frac{6}{10}$

(C) $\frac{5}{10}$ (D) $\frac{4}{10}$

5 What fraction of the squares are shaded?

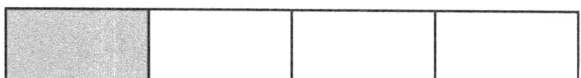

(A) $\frac{1}{4}$ (B) $\frac{2}{4}$

(C) $\frac{3}{4}$ (D) $\frac{4}{4}$

6 Fill in the missing numerator or denominator. $\frac{4}{8} = \frac{}{2}$

(A) 1   (B) 2   (C) 3   (D) 4

7 Fill in the missing numerator or denominator. $\frac{}{4} = \frac{6}{24}$

(A) 1   (B) 2   (C) 3   (D) 4

8 Fill in the missing numerator or denominator. $\frac{5}{} = \frac{8}{10}$

(A) 1   (B) 2   (C) 3   (D) 4

9 A pizza is cut into 12 equal slices. Chris ate 4 slices. What fraction of the pizza did Chris eat?

(A) $\frac{1}{4}$ (B) $\frac{2}{12}$ (C) $\frac{4}{12}$ (D) $\frac{5}{12}$

4.1 Dividing "A" Whole Into "B" Parts and A/B Fractions

---

10 There are 13 balls, 3 that are red. What fraction of the balls are red?

(A) $\frac{3}{13}$ (B) $\frac{2}{13}$ (C) $\frac{4}{13}$ (D) $\frac{5}{13}$

---

11 There are 7 pendant lights in the kitchen. Two of the bulbs are burned out. What fraction of the bulbs are burned out?

(A) $\frac{1}{7}$ (B) $\frac{2}{7}$ (C) $\frac{3}{7}$ (D) $\frac{5}{7}$

---

12 Eliza purchased 9 fish and 4 was golden fish. What fraction of the fish were golden?

(A) $\frac{1}{9}$ (B) $\frac{2}{9}$ (C) $\frac{8}{9}$ (D) $\frac{4}{9}$

---

13 There are 15 kids in a garden, 6 of them have black shoes. What fraction of the kids have black shoes?

(A) $\frac{15}{6}$ (B) $\frac{6}{15}$ (C) $\frac{5}{15}$ (D) $\frac{7}{15}$

---

14 Amy bought 5 animals, and one of them is a dog. What fraction of the animals are dogs?

(A) $\frac{1}{5}$ (B) $\frac{2}{5}$ (C) $\frac{3}{5}$ (D) $\frac{4}{5}$

15 Kiraz has 3 bedrooms in her house, and 2 of them are painted pink. What fraction of the bedrooms are pink?

(A) $\frac{1}{3}$ (B) $\frac{2}{3}$ (C) $\frac{3}{3}$ (D) $\frac{4}{3}$

16 Fill in the missing numerator or denominator. $\frac{2}{3} = \frac{14}{}$

(A) 7   (B) 14   (C) 9   (D) 18

17 Fill in the missing numerator or denominator. $\frac{}{5} = \frac{8}{10}$

(A) 7   (B) 4   (C) 3   (D) 2

18 What fraction of the squares are shaded?

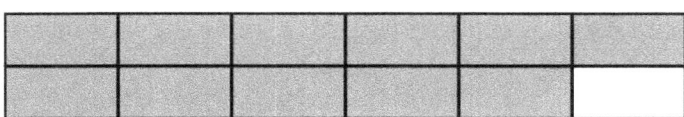

(A) $\frac{12}{11}$ (B) $\frac{8}{12}$ (C) $\frac{11}{12}$ (D) $\frac{9}{12}$

FRACTIONS

4.1 Dividing "A" Whole Into "B" Parts and A/B Fractions

19 Ann saw 9 tigers at the zoo. 3 of them was a white tiger. What fraction of the tigers were white tigers?

(A) $\frac{6}{9}$ (B) $\frac{9}{9}$ (C) $\frac{3}{9}$ (D) $\frac{2}{9}$

20 Fill in the missing numerator or denominator. $\frac{1}{7} = \frac{}{14}$

(A) 7   (B) 4   (C) 3   (D) 2

Next Section:
Fractions on The Number Line

FRACTIONS ON THE NUMBER LINE

A fraction is a means of writing a whole divided into a specific number of parts. Remember, a fraction consists of a numerator (the top number) and a denominator (the bottom number). The numerator contains the number of parts we have or care about. The denominator represents the total number of parts.

$$\frac{\text{numerator}}{\text{denominator}} = \frac{\text{number of parts we have or care}}{\text{aboutnumber of parts}}$$

One way to represent a fraction is to use a number line. This visual tool allows us to divide a whole into any number of equally sized pieces.

For example, the number line below shows how we would represent halves on the number line. When we consider halves, we are talking about dividing the whole into 2 equal parts. We can see on the number line that we have divided the region between 0 and 1 into 2 equal parts. The tick mark in the middle that divides our region is labeled $\frac{1}{2}$ because it indicates that from 0 to the tick mark is $\frac{1}{2}$ of the region.

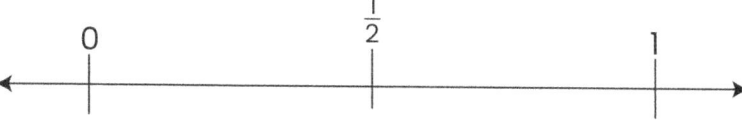

FRACTIONS ON THE NUMBER LINE

We can apply this same idea to regions that are divided into many more equal parts.

In the number line below, there are 7 tick marks to divide the region between 0 and 1 into 8 equal parts. As we move from 0 to 1, we can count the 8ths. The first tick mark is $\frac{1}{8}$, the second tick mark is $\frac{2}{8}$, and so on until we reach $\frac{8}{8}$ or 1.

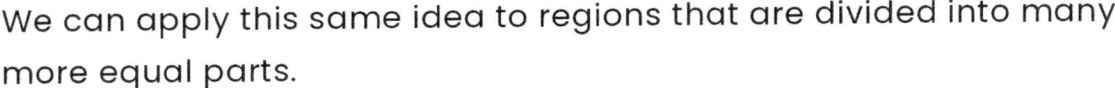
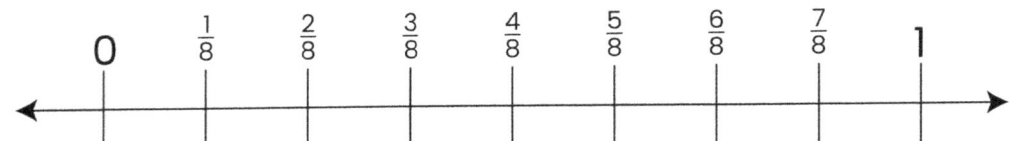

1 The library has 7 books on spirits. Romy checks out 5 of them. What fraction of the books did Romy check out?

(A) $\frac{6}{7}$ (B) $\frac{5}{7}$ (C) $\frac{4}{9}$ (D) $\frac{7}{8}$

2 Each of the last 10 years, Felix has purchased a new bag. In 6 of those years, her old bag was torn. What fraction of her old bag was torn?

(A) $\frac{5}{10}$ (B) $\frac{5}{7}$ (C) $\frac{4}{10}$ (D) $\frac{6}{10}$

3 Humans have 36 bones. Baby Sid has 25 of his own bones. What fraction of his bone does Baby Sid have?

(A) $\frac{36}{17}$ (B) $\frac{17}{36}$ (C) $\frac{15}{17}$ (D) $\frac{25}{36}$

4 A baker's dozen contains 15 doughnuts. Grace eats 8 doughnuts. What fraction of the baker's dozen did Grace eat?

(A) $\frac{9}{17}$ (B) $\frac{8}{13}$ (C) $\frac{13}{8}$ (D) $\frac{7}{13}$

5 A neighborhood park has 7 rings and a child has taken 2 rings. What fraction of rings are taken?

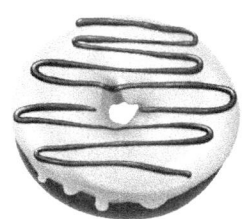

(A) $\frac{1}{7}$ (B) $\frac{2}{7}$ (C) $\frac{3}{7}$ (D) $\frac{5}{7}$

FRACTIONS

6   A box contained 20 apples, 1 which were rotten. What fraction of the apples are rotten?

(A) $\frac{1}{20}$ (B) $\frac{2}{20}$ (C) $\frac{5}{20}$ (D) $\frac{7}{20}$

7   There are 8 ice creams with John, and he ate 7 of them. What fraction of the ice creams have John eaten?

(A) $\frac{7}{8}$ (B) $\frac{2}{8}$ (C) $\frac{8}{9}$ (D) $\frac{7}{9}$

8   What fraction does the below number line represent on the dot?

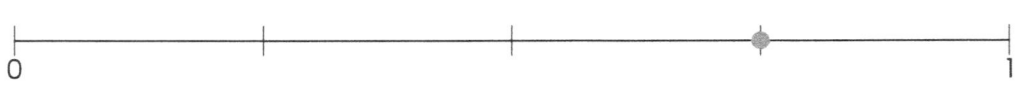

(A) $\frac{3}{4}$ (B) $\frac{2}{5}$ (C) $\frac{2}{4}$ (D) $\frac{1}{4}$

9   What fraction does the dot represent?

(A) $\frac{7}{8}$ (B) $\frac{6}{8}$ (C) $\frac{5}{8}$ (D) $\frac{3}{8}$

10 What fraction does the dot represent?

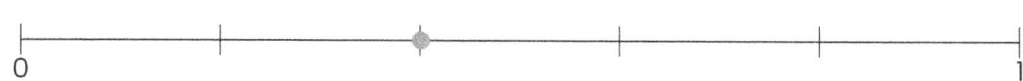

(A) $\frac{3}{5}$ (B) $\frac{2}{5}$ (C) $\frac{4}{5}$ (D) $\frac{1}{5}$

11 What fraction does the below number line represent on the dot?

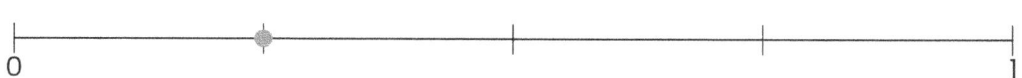

(A) $\frac{3}{4}$ (B) $\frac{2}{5}$ (C) $\frac{2}{4}$ (D) $\frac{1}{4}$

12 What fraction does the dot represent?

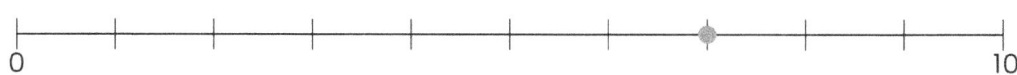

(A) $\frac{6}{10}$ (B) $\frac{5}{10}$ (C) $\frac{8}{10}$ (D) $\frac{7}{10}$

13 What fraction does the dot represent?

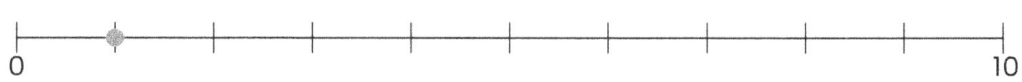

(A) $\frac{6}{10}$ (B) $\frac{5}{10}$ (C) $\frac{1}{10}$ (D) $\frac{7}{10}$

FRACTIONS

4.2 Fractions on The Number Line

14 What fraction does the dot represent?

(A) $\frac{16}{20}$ (B) $\frac{15}{20}$ (C) $\frac{1}{20}$ (D) $\frac{17}{20}$

15 What fraction does the dot represent?

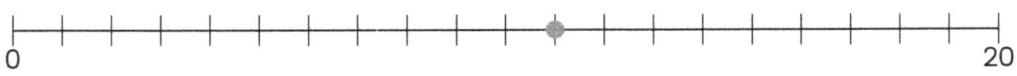

(A) $\frac{16}{20}$ (B) $\frac{7}{20}$ (C) $\frac{10}{20}$ (D) $\frac{17}{20}$

16 There are 12 kids attending a campout, and 3 of them have blue hats. What fraction of the kids have blue hats?

(A) $\frac{4}{12}$ (B) $\frac{3}{12}$ (C) $\frac{6}{12}$ (D) $\frac{7}{12}$

17 Matt watched 5 movies, out of which 3 were thriller movies. What fraction of the movies watched are thrillers?

(A) $\frac{2}{5}$ (B) $\frac{3}{5}$ (C) $\frac{1}{5}$ (D) $\frac{5}{6}$

18 In an exhibition, Jenny made 30 sandwiches and sold 13 of them. What fraction of sandwiches did she sell?

(A) $\frac{13}{30}$ (B) $\frac{23}{30}$ (C) $\frac{17}{30}$ (D) $\frac{13}{20}$

19 Eda read 11 novels, out of which 7 are comic books. What fraction of the comic novels watched are thrillers?

(A) $\frac{7}{11}$ (B) $\frac{9}{11}$ (C) $\frac{5}{11}$ (D) $\frac{2}{1}$

20 There are 33 oranges in a basket. 17 of them are rotten. What fraction of oranges are rotten?

(A) $\frac{17}{33}$ (B) $\frac{17}{30}$ (C) $\frac{15}{33}$ (D) $\frac{1}{33}$

Next Section: Equivalent Fractions

EQUIVALENT FRACTIONS

Equivalent fractions are fractions that have the same value, but may be written using different numbers. For example, the fractions $\frac{1}{2}$ and $\frac{2}{4}$ are equivalent because they represent the same amount. If we cut a pizza in half, we have 2 parts. If we eat one half of the pizza, we write this as $\frac{1}{2}$. We could also cut the pizza into 4 slices. In order to eat half of the pizza, we'd have to eat 2 slices. We write this as $\frac{2}{4}$. Even though the numbers in the fractions are different, the amount of pizza represented is the same.

Example:

Write an equivalent fraction for $\frac{2}{3}$.

We must multiply the numerator and the denominator by a factor. This factor can be any number. We'll pick 2

$$\frac{2 \times 2}{3 \times 2} = \frac{4}{6}$$

$$\frac{4}{6} = \frac{2}{3}$$

1   Select the fraction that is *not* equivalent. $\frac{1}{4}$

(A) $\frac{2}{8}$ (B) $\frac{4}{16}$ (C) $\frac{2}{4}$ (D) $\frac{3}{12}$

2   Select the fraction that is *not* equivalent. $\frac{2}{5}$

(A) $\frac{4}{10}$ (B) $\frac{6}{15}$ (C) $\frac{4}{5}$ (D) $\frac{8}{20}$

3   Fill in the blank with the missing numerator or denominator. $\frac{1}{3} = \frac{}{9}$

(A) 3   (B) 4   (C) 2   (D) 5

4   Fill in the blank with the missing numerator or denominator. $\frac{3}{} = \frac{15}{25}$

(A) 3   (B) 4   (C) 2   (D) 5

5   Fill in the blank with the missing numerator or denominator. $\frac{4}{} = \frac{2}{5}$

(A) 3   (B) 10   (C) 8   (D) 5

FRACTIONS

6 Fill in the blank with the missing numerator or denominator. $\frac{4}{5} = \frac{12}{-}$

(A) 15   (B) 3   (C) 18   (D) 5

7 Determine whether the fractions are equal or not. $\frac{5}{7} = \frac{10}{14}$

(A) Equal   (B) Not Equal

8 Determine whether the fractions are equal or not. $\frac{2}{3} = \frac{4}{7}$

(A) Equal   (B) Not Equal

9 There are 12 slices of bread. Eda ate 3 slices; compute the fraction of slices she consumed with a denominators of 6.

(A) $\frac{1}{5}$ (B) $\frac{1}{6}$ (C) $\frac{1}{2}$ (D) $\frac{2}{3}$

10 In a group of 15 people, 5 have the same network provider. Write the fraction of people with the same network provider with a denominator of 30.

(A) $\frac{10}{30}$ (B) $\frac{20}{30}$ (C) $\frac{5}{30}$ (D) $\frac{12}{20}$

11 There are 9 fruit pouches. Matt ate 4 of them. Write the fraction of pouches eaten with a numerator of 8.

(A) $\frac{8}{18}$ (B) $\frac{8}{20}$ (C) $\frac{8}{10}$ (D) $\frac{8}{7}$

12 There are 27 cars in the parking lot, and 3 of them are Innovas. Write the fraction of Innova in the parking lot with a numerator of 1.

(A) $\frac{1}{5}$ (B) $\frac{1}{9}$ (C) $\frac{1}{10}$ (D) $\frac{1}{7}$

13 A Park has 4 swings occupied out of the 14 in the building. Write the fraction of working treadmills with a numerator of 2.

(A) $\frac{2}{3}$ (B) $\frac{2}{7}$ (C) $\frac{2}{5}$ (D) $\frac{2}{6}$

14 A football team has 13 players, and 5 most of them are brown-haired. Write the fraction of brown-haired players with a denominator of 26.

(A) $\frac{10}{26}$ (B) $\frac{15}{26}$ (C) $\frac{20}{26}$ (D) $\frac{7}{26}$

15 There are 48 houses in a neighborhood, and 18 of the houses have white tiles. Write the fraction of houses that white tiles with a denominator of 8.

(A) $\frac{7}{3}$ (B) $\frac{8}{3}$ (C) $\frac{3}{8}$ (D) $\frac{2}{3}$

FRACTIONS

Equivalent Fractions

16 Fill in the blank with the missing numerator or denominator. $\frac{5}{9} = \frac{35}{\_\_}$

(A) 63   (B) 70   (C) 81   (D) 55

17 Fill in the blank with the missing numerator or denominator. $\frac{8}{14} = \frac{4}{\_\_}$

(A) 5   (B) 7   (C) 8   (D) 9

18 Determine whether the factions are equal or not. $\frac{2}{7} = \frac{4}{11}$

(A) Equal   (B) Not Equal

19 A building has 80 flats, and 30 of them are vacant. Write the fraction of vacant flats with a denominator of 6.

(A) $\frac{20}{6}$ (B) $\frac{16}{6}$ (C) $\frac{9}{6}$ (D) $\frac{11}{6}$

20 Linda has 18 dresses, and 6 of them are red. Write the fraction of the red dress with a numerator of 1.

(A) $\frac{1}{2}$ (B) $\frac{1}{6}$

(C) $\frac{1}{3}$ (D) $\frac{1}{5}$

Next Section: Express Whole Numbers As Fractions

EXPRESS WHOLE NUMBERS AS FRACTIONS

Fractions are a way to express parts of a whole. Sometimes a part of a whole equals the whole. When this happens, we are expressing a whole number as a fraction.

We can represent the number 1 in infinitely many ways. For example, the rectangle below has been divided into 4 equal parts, and each part is shaded.

When writing this as a fraction, we write the number of parts we have, 4, over the total number of equal parts, 4, which gives $\frac{4}{4}$.

We only have the 1 whole block (that has been divided into equal parts), so we know $1 = \frac{4}{4}$.

EXPRESS WHOLE NUMBERS AS FRACTIONS

Let's increase the complexity slightly and represent the whole number 3 as a fraction. There are 3 circles below that have each been divided into 4 equal parts.

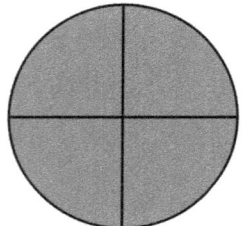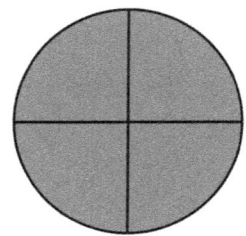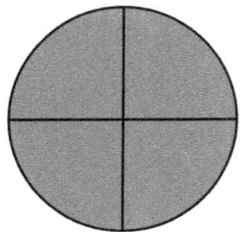

We count the number of shaded parts of the circles and arrive at a total of 12. To write this as a fraction, we write it over the number of equal parts in each circle, 4. Therefore, we can represent the whole number 3 as $\frac{12}{4}$.

We can also write any whole number as a fraction with a denominator of 1.

Express Whole Numbers As Fractions   4.4

1 Write the whole number as a fraction with a denominator of 1.

77

(A) $\frac{77}{1}$ (B) $\frac{72}{1}$ (C) $\frac{70}{1}$ (D) $\frac{76}{1}$

2 Write the whole number as a fraction with a denominator of 1.

16

(A) $\frac{14}{1}$ (B) $\frac{16}{1}$ (C) $\frac{2}{1}$ (D) $\frac{26}{1}$

3 Write the whole number as a fraction with a denominator of 4.

5

(A) $\frac{14}{4}$ (B) $\frac{10}{4}$ (C) $\frac{20}{4}$ (D) $\frac{26}{4}$

4 Write the whole number as a fraction with a denominator of 3.

21

(A) $\frac{60}{3}$ (B) $\frac{63}{3}$ (C) $\frac{75}{3}$ (D) $\frac{66}{3}$

5 Use the pictures to write the whole number as a fraction.

(A) $\frac{6}{2}$ (B) $\frac{6}{3}$ (C) $\frac{12}{6}$ (D) $\frac{12}{3}$

4.4 Express Whole Numbers As Fractions

6 Use the pictures to write the whole number as a fraction.

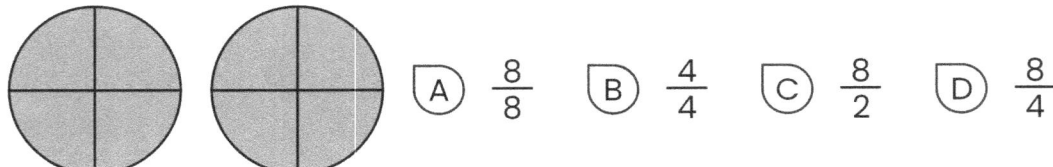

(A) $\frac{8}{8}$ (B) $\frac{4}{4}$ (C) $\frac{8}{2}$ (D) $\frac{8}{4}$

7 Use the pictures to write the whole number as a fraction.

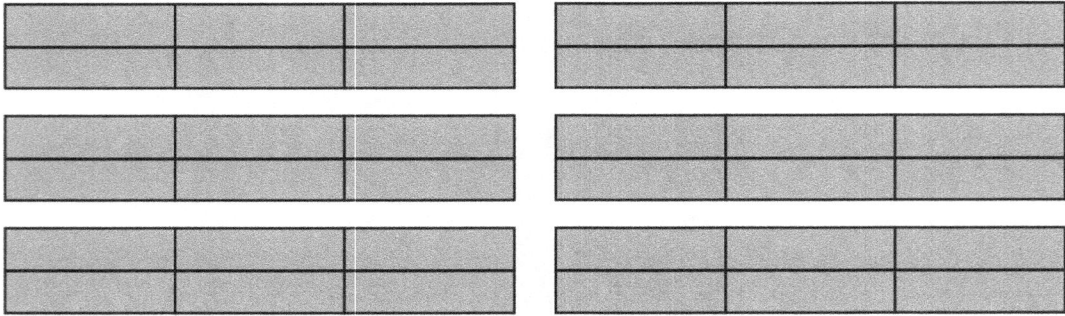

(A) $\frac{30}{5}$ (B) $\frac{24}{6}$ (C) $\frac{18}{6}$ (D) $\frac{36}{6}$

8 Robert ate 5 sandwiches. Each sandwich had 4 sliced. Write the number of sandwiches as a fractions, using slices as the parts.

(A) $\frac{20}{4}$ (B) $\frac{25}{4}$ (C) $\frac{16}{4}$ (D) $\frac{12}{4}$

Express Whole Numbers As Fractions **4.4**

9 There are 6 boxes. A box has 12 chocolates. Write the number of chocolates in a box as a fraction.

(A) $\frac{60}{12}$ (B) $\frac{56}{12}$ (C) $\frac{72}{12}$ (D) $\frac{82}{12}$

10 A basket has 15 packs of balls. In each back, 9 balls are green. Write the number of green balls using the number of balls as the parts.

(A) $\frac{135}{15}$ (B) $\frac{155}{9}$ (C) $\frac{140}{15}$ (D) $\frac{129}{9}$

11 One cup contains 14 cubes of sugar. Lisa took 5 cups of sugar and used them in a recipe. Write the number of cubes of sugar as a fraction, using the cubes used as the parts.

(A) $\frac{60}{5}$ (B) $\frac{70}{5}$ (C) $\frac{82}{5}$ (D) $\frac{65}{5}$

12 There are 12 months in a year. Write 4 years as a fraction using months as the parts.

(A) $\frac{12}{4}$ (B) $\frac{48}{4}$ (C) $\frac{4}{12}$ (D) $\frac{48}{12}$

FRACTIONS

4.4   **Express Whole Numbers As Fractions**

13   Write the number 6 as a fraction with a denominator of 5.

(A) $\frac{35}{5}$ (B) $\frac{30}{5}$ (C) $\frac{44}{5}$ (D) $\frac{48}{5}$

14   Write the number 10 as a fraction with a denominator of 1.

(A) $\frac{2}{1}$ (B) $\frac{15}{1}$ (C) $\frac{11}{1}$ (D) $\frac{10}{1}$

15   Use the pictures to write the whole number as a fraction.

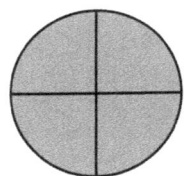 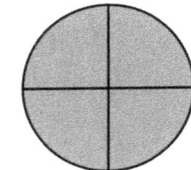 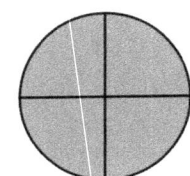 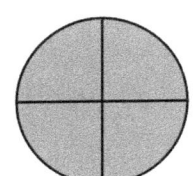

(A) $\frac{8}{4}$ (B) $\frac{16}{4}$ (C) $\frac{12}{4}$ (D) $\frac{10}{4}$

16   A bag contains 10 packs. Each pack contains 4 toys. Write the number of bags as a fraction using the pack of toys as the parts.

(A) $\frac{30}{4}$ (B) $\frac{10}{4}$ (C) $\frac{40}{4}$ (D) $\frac{20}{4}$

Express Whole Numbers As Fractions   4.4

17 Write the whole number as a fraction with a denominator of 9.

9

(A) $\frac{81}{9}$ (B) $\frac{72}{9}$ (C) $\frac{63}{9}$ (D) $\frac{83}{9}$

18 Use the pictures to write the whole number as a fraction.

(A) $\frac{10}{3}$ (B) $\frac{13}{3}$ (C) $\frac{9}{9}$ (D) $\frac{9}{3}$

19 There are 5 boxes. A box has 10 cookies. Write the number of cookies in a box as a fraction.

(A) $\frac{50}{10}$ (B) $\frac{56}{10}$ (C) $\frac{72}{10}$ (D) $\frac{82}{10}$

20 Write the number 29 as a fraction with a denominator of 1.

(A) $\frac{29}{1}$ (B) $\frac{30}{1}$ (C) $\frac{44}{1}$ (D) $\frac{48}{1}$

Next Section:
Compare The Fractions

COMPARE THE FRACTIONS

Compare fractions that either have the same numerator or the same denominator.

If two fractions have the same denominator, the fraction with the *larger* numerator is bigger.

If two fractions have the same numerator, the fraction with the *smaller* denominator is bigger.

Example:

Which is bigger: $\frac{3}{8}$ or $\frac{5}{8}$

It helps to draw the whole and the shaded parts to make the comparison.

We see from the pictures that $\frac{5}{8}$ has more of the whole shaded. Therefore, we know $\frac{3}{8} < \frac{5}{8}$.

1   Fill in >,<or = to make the statement true. $\frac{8}{9}$ _____ $\frac{8}{11}$

2   Fill in >,<or = to make the statement true. $\frac{12}{7}$ _____ $\frac{12}{6}$

3   Fill in >,<or = to make the statement true. $\frac{5}{4}$ _____ $\frac{6}{4}$

4   Fill in >,<or = to make the statement true. $\frac{13}{7}$ _____ $\frac{11}{7}$

5   Fill in >,<or = to make the statement true. $\frac{15}{9}$ _____ $\frac{15}{9}$

6   Select the fraction that makes the statement true. $\frac{1}{9}$ > _____.

(A) $\frac{1}{8}$ (B) $\frac{1}{10}$ (C) $\frac{2}{9}$ (D) $\frac{1}{6}$

7   Select the fraction that makes the statement true. $\frac{8}{7}$ < _____.

(A) $\frac{5}{9}$ (B) $\frac{6}{7}$ (C) $\frac{2}{9}$ (D) $\frac{9}{5}$

4.5 **Compare The Fractions**

8 Select the fraction that makes the statement true. $\frac{4}{7} >$ _____.

(A) $\frac{5}{7}$ (B) $\frac{4}{8}$ (C) $\frac{2}{9}$ (D) $\frac{9}{5}$

9 Allen ate $\frac{4}{8}$ of a wrap, and Aaron ate $\frac{3}{8}$. Who ate more wrap?

(A) Allen   (B) Aaron

10 Robert completed $\frac{7}{4}$ of Homework and Stella completed $\frac{7}{9}$ of homework. Who completed more homework?

(A) Robert   (B) Stella

11 Yesterday, Stephen walked $\frac{5}{7}$, and today he walked $\frac{5}{8}$. Did he walk more on yesterday or today?

(A) Today   (B) Yesterday

12 On Monday, Juan ate $\frac{9}{8}$ of pizza. On Tuesday, he ate $\frac{6}{8}$. On which day did he eat more?

(A) Monday   (B) Tuesday

13 Jeremy completed $\frac{4}{15}$ of an obstacle course, and Tom completed $\frac{4}{19}$ of the same obstacle course. Who completed more of the course?

(A) Jeremy   (B) Tom

14 Stephen doesn't like to run. His coach says group A will run $\frac{10}{9}$ of the trail and the other group B will run $\frac{12}{9}$ of the train Which group should he choose?

(A) Group A   (B) Group B

15 Fill in >,<or = to make the statement true. $\frac{35}{14}$ _____ $\frac{30}{14}$

16 Fill in >,<or = to make the statement true. $\frac{11}{9}$ _____ $\frac{11}{5}$

17 Den completed $\frac{4}{2}$ laps around the track while Donald completed $\frac{4}{5}$ laps around the track. Who completed fewer laps?

(A) Den   (B) Donald

4.5   **Compare The Fractions**

18   Select the fraction that makes the statement true. $\dfrac{11}{6} <$ _____.

   (A) $\dfrac{11}{5}$ (B) $\dfrac{11}{2}$ (C) $\dfrac{12}{5}$ (D) $\dfrac{9}{5}$

19   Select the fraction that makes the statement true. $\dfrac{4}{9} >$ _____.

   (A) $\dfrac{2}{9}$ (B) $\dfrac{5}{9}$ (C) $\dfrac{5}{5}$ (D) $\dfrac{6}{5}$

20   Select the fraction that makes the statement true. $\dfrac{3}{7} =$ _____.

   (A) $\dfrac{2}{7}$ (B) $\dfrac{3}{7}$ (C) $\dfrac{4}{7}$ (D) $\dfrac{6}{7}$

Next Section: Chapter Review

1   What is the denominator of the fraction? $\frac{2}{5}$

(A) 1   (B) 2   (C) 3   (D) 5

2   What is the denominator of the fraction? $\frac{6}{5}$

(A) 6   (B) 5   (C) 3   (D) 4

3   What fraction of the squares are shaded?

(A) $\frac{2}{5}$ (B) $\frac{3}{5}$ (C) $\frac{4}{5}$ (D) $\frac{3}{5}$

4   Of the 17 Carrots, 7 that are damaged. What fraction of the carrots are damaged?

(A) $\frac{3}{17}$ (B) $\frac{5}{17}$ (C) $\frac{7}{17}$ (D) $\frac{10}{17}$

5   Fill in the missing numerator or denominator. $\frac{5}{9} = \frac{10}{}$

(A) 25   (B) 21   (C) 9   (D) 18

FRACTIONS

6 The library has 20 books on history. Jenny checks out 11 of them. What fraction of the books did Jenny check out?

(A) $\frac{15}{20}$ (B) $\frac{11}{20}$ (C) $\frac{18}{20}$ (D) $\frac{9}{20}$

7 A box had 35 dates and 5 of them were rotten. What fraction of the dates are rotten?

(A) $\frac{1}{35}$ (B) $\frac{2}{35}$ (C) $\frac{5}{35}$ (D) $\frac{7}{35}$

8 There are 18 kids attending a campout, and 5 of them have black bags. What fraction of the kids have black bags?

(A) $\frac{4}{18}$ (B) $\frac{5}{18}$ (C) $\frac{6}{18}$ (D) $\frac{7}{18}$

9 In an Exhibition, Nilofer makes 15 pizzas. She sold 5 of them. What fraction of pizzas did she sell?

(A) $\frac{13}{15}$ (B) $\frac{5}{15}$ (C) $\frac{7}{15}$ (D) $\frac{11}{15}$

10 There are 55 watermelons in a basket. 25 of them are rotten. What fraction of watermelons are rotten?

(A) $\frac{25}{55}$ (B) $\frac{17}{55}$ (C) $\frac{36}{55}$ (D) $\frac{15}{55}$

11   Select the fraction that is not equivalent. $\dfrac{6}{7}$

(A) $\dfrac{12}{14}$ (B) $\dfrac{18}{21}$ (C) $\dfrac{12}{7}$ (D) $\dfrac{24}{28}$

12   Fill in the blank with the missing numerator or denominator. $\dfrac{4}{\quad} = \dfrac{8}{18}$

(A) 2   (B) 4   (C) 9   (D) 5

13   Determine whether the fractions are equal or not. $\dfrac{6}{5} = \dfrac{12}{14}$

(A) Equal   (B) Not Equal

14   There are 15 fruit pouches. Chris ate 3 of them. Write the fraction of pouches eaten with a numerators of 6.

(A) $\dfrac{6}{18}$ (B) $\dfrac{6}{30}$ (C) $\dfrac{6}{10}$ (D) $\dfrac{6}{7}$

15   Determine whether the factions are equal or not. $\dfrac{5}{6} = \dfrac{15}{18}$

(A) Equal   (B) Not Equal

16   Write the whole number as a fraction with a denominator of 1.

                                                           100

(A) $\dfrac{100}{1}$ (B) $\dfrac{1}{100}$ (C) $\dfrac{70}{1}$ (D) $\dfrac{76}{1}$

4.6 **Chapter Review**

17 Write the whole number as a fraction with a denominator of 5.

13

(A) $\frac{60}{5}$ (B) $\frac{63}{5}$ (C) $\frac{65}{5}$ (D) $\frac{66}{5}$

18 Use the pictures to write the whole number as a fraction.

(A) $\frac{12}{2}$ (B) $\frac{6}{3}$ (C) $\frac{12}{4}$ (D) $\frac{12}{3}$

19 There are 5 boxes. A box has 10 cookies. Write the number of cookies in a box as a fraction.

(A) $\frac{50}{10}$ (B) $\frac{56}{10}$ (C) $\frac{72}{10}$ (D) $\frac{82}{10}$

20 Write the number 3 as a fraction with a denominator of 7.

(A) $\frac{21}{7}$ (B) $\frac{30}{7}$ (C) $\frac{44}{7}$ (D) $\frac{48}{7}$

Next Chapter: Measurement ≫

CHAPTER 5

MEASUREMENT

COMPLETE THE PATTERN

 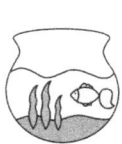   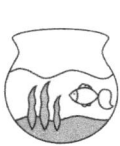

TIME INTERVALS TO THE NEAREST MINUTE

Time can be measured in many different ways. We refer to time as years, months, weeks, days, hours and minutes. Each interval of time is built on a smaller unit of time. 60 minutes is one hour; 7 days is one week; 52 weeks is one year.

Typically, we measure time (hours and minutes) on a clock. An analog clock displays the time using an hour (short) and a minute (long) hand. The short hand indicates the hour, and the long hand indicates the minutes. We can also display the time on a number line. Remember, since there are 60 minutes in an hour, the spacing between our hour marks should represent 60 minutes.

The clocks below show the time 12:47 on both an analog clock and a number line.

We can also add or subtract time. To add time, we add the hours to the hours and the minutes to the minutes. If the minutes exceed 60, we subtract 60 from the minutes and add 1 to the hours.

If the hours are greater than 12, we subtract 12. To subtract time, we subtract the hours from the hours and the minutes from the minutes. If the minutes are negative, we add 60 to the minutes and subtract 1 from the hours. If the hours are negative, we add 12.

TIME INTERVALS TO THE NEAREST MINUTE

Example:

What is 8:47 + 2:29 = ?

First, we add the hours: 8 + 2 = 10.

Then we add the minutes: 47 + 29 = 76.

Since the minutes are greater than 60, we subtract 60: 76 - 60 = 16.

Since the minutes are greater than 60, we add 1 to the hours: 10 + 1 = 11.

Then, we combine the hours and minutes for the time: 11:16.

Time Intervals to The Nearest Minute   5.1

1   What time does the clock show?

(A) Two after three   (B) Two o'clock

(C) Two to three   (D) Twenty-three

2   What time does the clock show?

(A) 1:09   (B) 9:01   (C) 1:45   (D) 9:05

3   What time does the clock show?

(A) Nine o'clock   (B) Forty-five past nine

(C) Nine   (D) Forty-five

4   Lisa set her alarm to go off so she could complete homework and get to school on time. Is it AM or PM?

(A) A.M   (B) P.M

MEASUREMENT

5.1   Time Intervals to The Nearest Minute

5   The school bus arrives at the stop at 6:50 each morning, and it takes Rocky 5 minutes to walk to the stop. What time should Rocky leave his house each morning?

   (A) 6:40   (B) 6:55   (C) 5:45   (D) 6:45

6   Which digital clock shows the same time as this analog clock?

(A)  06:19   (B)  12:53

(C)  10:38   (D)  07:58

7   Remy's math class starts at 10:45 and lasts 45 minutes. What time does his math class end?

   (A) 11:30   (B) 11:55   (C) 11:45   (D) 10:55

8   It takes Mia 56 minutes to clean the first floor of her house. If she starts cleaning, 1:35 what time will she finish?

   (A) 02:30   (B) 02:31   (C) 02:35   (D) 02:56

9 Lee drives for 23 minutes to reach his office. He leaves his house at 8:25. What time does he arrived at the office?

(A) 07:38   (B) 09:55   (C) 08:48   (D) 11:55

10 The math test begins at 3:00 p.m. The last student finishes after 37 minutes. At what time did the last student finish?

_____

11 Select the analog clock that displays the same time as the timeline.

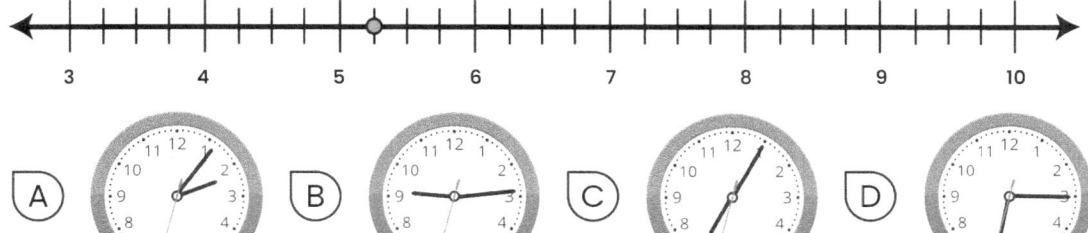

(A)   (B)   (C)   (D)

12 Determine the amount of time that has elapsed.
Start: 8:46, Stop: 12:12

(A) 02:46   (B) 03:26

(C) 09:35   (D) 11:56

MEASUREMENT

5.1 Time Intervals to The Nearest Minute

13 What is 7:54 - 2:09 = ?

(A) 06:26   (B) 07:16   (C) 05:09   (D) 04:45

14 A cake must bake for 44 minutes. Amy puts her cake in the oven at 2:21. At what time will her cake be done?

_____

15 It takes David 55 minutes to finish his fishing. He went to a fishing spot at 10:40. What time did he finish fishing?

(A) 12:06   (B) 12:16   (C) 11:35   (D) 11:46

16 A basketball game lasts 2 hours 13 minutes. The game started at 05:20. What time did the game finish?

(A) 06:56   (B) 07:33   (C) 08:43   (D) 09:36

17 Lexi takes 3 hours 30 minutes to complete her homework. She starts to do her homework at 05:00. At what time does Lexi complete her homework?

(A) 08:30   (B) 06:40   (C) 09:20   (D) 05:30

18 Claudia cooks for 2 hours 27 minutes. She started cooking at 12:10. What time did she stop cooking?

_____

19 Russell painted his bedroom for 4 hours 10 minutes. He starts to paint at 8:51. At what time did he finish painting?

(A) 11:10   (B) 12:51   (C) 01:01   (D) 01:51

20 Jeff watched television for 1 hour 17 minutes. He switched off the television at 2:37. At what time does he switch on the television?

(A) 01:20   (B) 02:54   (C) 03:37   (D) 01:17

Next Chapter: Estimate Liquid Volumes and Masses

ESTIMATE LIQUID VOLUMES AND MASSES

Volume is a measure of the capacity of an object, or how much it can hold. We measure volume in liters or milliliters. Mass is a measure of how heavy something is. We measure mass in grams and kilograms.

A liter is equal to 1000 milliliters. When we measure or estimate the capacity of an object, we choose the units based on our knowledge. A milliliter is equal to a few 20 drops of rain, so when we are dealing with the volume or capacity of a small object, we should measure it in milliliters. When dealing with objects of larger capacity, we measure the volume in liters. For example, we would measure a bucket of water in liters, but a medicine dropper in milliliters.

Kilograms and grams are used to measure the mass of an object. A kilogram is equal to 1000 grams. Unlike with volume, the size of an object is irrelevant to its mass. For example, the feather of a bird has a mass of 0.0082 grams. On the other hand, a one-inch sphere of lead has a mass of 98 grams. When we think about the mass of an object, we must consider how much matter the object contains.

We use grams to measure the mass of objects with small amounts of matter (like a feather) and kilograms to measure the mass of objects with large amounts of matter (like books or cars).

1 To measure the mass of a bus we should use ?

(A) Liters   (B) Milliliters   (C) Grams   (D) Kilograms

2 To measure the mass of a pen we should use ?

(A) Liters   (B) Milliliters   (C) Grams   (D) Kilograms

3 To measure the volume of a raindrop we should use ?

(A) Liters   (B) Milliliters   (C) Grams   (D) Kilograms

4 To measure the volume of water in a barrel we should use ?

(A) Liters   (B) Milliliters   (C) Grams   (D) Kilograms

5 The volume of a tall juice glass is approximately
_____.

(A) 2 ml   (B) 350 ml   (C) 10 g   (D) 1 L

MEASUREMENT

5.2 Estimate Liquid Volumes and Masses

6 The mass of a toothbrush is approximately _____.

A) 1 kg   B) 45 ml   C) 18 g   D) 3 L

7 Tom brings apples and oranges. What unit should he use to measure the mass of apples and oranges?

A) Liters   B) Milliliters   C) Grams   D) Kilograms

8 Zara fills her tank with water. What unit should she use to measure the volume of her tank?

A) Liters   B) Milliliters   C) Grams   D) Kilograms

9 Adam bought a white rose from a flower shop. What unit should be used to measure a red rose?

A) Liters   B) Milliliters   C) Grams   D) Kilograms

10 Sam purchased 5 packs of sugar. What unit should be used to measure the total amount of sugar in the packs?

A) Liters   B) Milliliters   C) Grams   D) Kilograms

11 Eric bought a ring from a shop. What unit should be used to measure the ring?

(A) Grams   (B) Kilograms   (C) Liters   (D) Milliliters

12 What unit should be used to measure the volume of an oil can?

(A) Grams   (B) Kilograms   (C) Liters   (D) Milliliters

13 Smith drives a school van. What unit should be used to measure the school van?

(A) Grams   (B) Kilograms   (C) Liters   (D) Milliliters

14 To measure the mass of a watermelon we should use ?

(A) Liters   (B) Milliliters   (C) Grams   (D) Kilograms

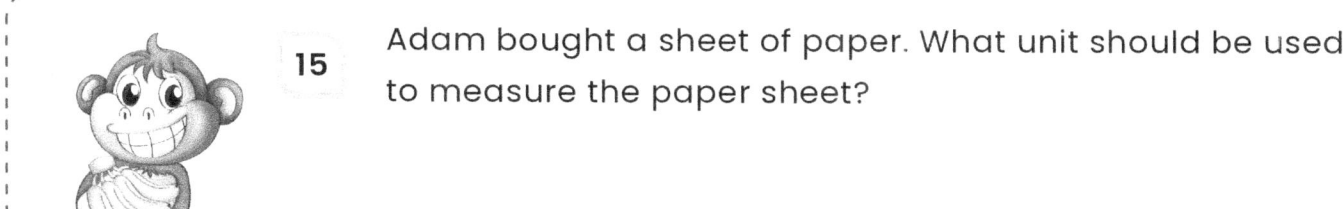

15 Adam bought a sheet of paper. What unit should be used to measure the paper sheet?

_____

5.2 Estimate liquid volumes and masses

16 Annie fills a large bucket with water. What unit should be used to measure the water in a bucket?

(A) Grams   (B) Kilograms   (C) Liters   (D) Milliliters

17 Elena drinks a cup of coffee. What unit should be used to measure the volume of a coffee cup?

(A) Liters   (B) Milliliters   (C) Grams   (D) Kilograms

18 The volume of water glass is approximately _____.

(A) 3 ml   (B) 250 ml   (C) 50 g   (D) 7 L

19 The mass of a small stone is approximately _____.

(A) 4 kg   (B) 15 ml   (C) 7 g   (D) 2 L

20 The mass of a smartphone should be measured in what unit?

(A) Grams   (B) Kilograms   (C) Liters   (D) Milliliters

Next Section: Add and Subtract Involving Masses or Volumes

ADD AND SUBTRACT INVOLVING MASSES OR VOLUMES

We can add and subtract masses and volumes as long as the units are the same. We can add grams to grams, kilograms to kilograms, liters to liters, and milliliters to milliliters. We cannot, for example, add kilograms and milliliters.

When adding or subtracting masses and volumes, we treat the values as regular numbers and complete the operation. Then, when reporting our answer, we attach the unit.

Example:

A serving of cheese is 114 grams and a serving of crackers is 188 grams. If John eats a serving of cheese and a serving of crackers, how many grams of food did he eat?

We add the mass of the cheese and the crackers:

114 + 188 = 100 + 10 + 4 + 100 + 80 + 8 = 200 + 90 + 12 = 300 + 2 = 302.

Then, we add the unit to our solution: 302 grams

MEASUREMENT

5.3 Add and Subtract Involving Masses or Volumes

1 Dallas makes orange juice. She adds 255 ml of water and 173 ml of orange juice. How much water and orange juice did she have in total?

(A) 355 ml   (B) 428 ml   (C) 473 ml   (D) 397 ml

2 Hailey measured out three spoonfuls of sugar. The first spoonful measured 13 grams, the second spoonful measures 16 grams, and the third spoonful measures 19 grams. How much total mass do the three spoonfuls have?

(A) 37 grams   (B) 40 grams   (C) 48 grams   (D) 52 grams

3 Gail fills the small swimming pool with 893 liters of water. He then decides to add 97 liters of water. How much water is in the swimming pool?

(A) 990 liters   (B) 999 liters   (C) 897 liters (D) 797 liters

4 Jerry is drinking a 510 ml bottle of milk. After a single sip, there are 457 ml left. How much did he drink?

(A) 41 ml   (B) 49 ml   (C) 53 ml   (D) 57 ml

5 A male and female lion in a cage. The male lion weighs 188 kg, and the female lion weighs 126 kg. How much do both lions weigh combined?

(A) 365 kg   (B) 254 kg   (C) 289 kg   (D) 314 kg

6 Joy is making ice cream. He measured out 312 ml of thickened cream and 157 ml of milk. How much cream and milk are in her bowl?

(A) 408 ml   (B) 445 ml   (C) 469 ml   (D) 477 ml

7 A dining table weighs 78 kg, and a chair weighs 21 kg. How much more does a dining table weigh than a chair?

(A) 44 kg   (B) 57 kg   (C) 63 kg   (D) 79 kg

8 Leo uses 22 L water to clean his bike. Mario uses 63 L water to clean his car. How much more water does Mario use than Leo?

(A) 50 liters   (B) 99 liters   (C) 89 liters   (D) 41 liters

9 Ben is carrying two small bags. The first bag is 432 g and the second bag is 486 g. How many bags is Ben carrying?

(A) 918 grams   (B) 987 grams
(C) 886 grams   (D) 832 grams

MEASUREMENT

5.3   **Add and Subtract Involving Masses or Volumes**

10 The old water tank holds 398 L water. The new water tank holds 543 L water. How much more water does the new water tank hold than the old water tank?

(A) 153 liters   (B) 167 liters   (C) 145 liters   (D) 176 liters

11 A rectangle-shaped carpet has a mass of 55 kg, and a square-shaped carpet has a mass of 47 kg. What is the mass of both a rectangle and a square carpet?

_____

12 The car engine has a mass of 939 kg, and the motorcycle engine has a mass of 257 kg. How much more mass does the car engine have than a motorcycle?

_____

13 Lily bought 750g of flour and 500g of sugar. How much more flour does Lily need more than sugar?

(A) 200 grams   (B) 250 grams

(C) 300 grams   (D) 350 grams

14 Anika has 377 kg teddy bears and 491 kg Barbie dolls. What is the combined mass of teddy bears and Barbie dolls?

(A) 698 kg   (B) 754 kg   (C) 791 kg   (D) 868 kg

15 A full pizza is 255 grams, but Demi eats 115 grams. How many grams are left?

(A) 140 grams   (B) 176 grams   (C) 181 grams   (D) 197 grams

16 Diego's weight is 76 kg, and Luke's weight is 87 kg. What is their total weight?

(A) 209 kg   (B) 154 kg   (C) 163 kg   (D) 211 kg

17 A bottle contains 758 mL water. Jaxon drank 324 mL water. How much water is left in the bottle?

_____

MEASUREMENT

5.3   **Add and Subtract Involving Masses or Volumes**

18   To determine how many apples are sold each day, a store weighs the apples before they open and after they close. On Monday, there are 876 kg apples before opening and 289 kg after closing. How many kilograms of apples were sold that day?

_____

19   Austin sells soda. On Saturday, he sold 371 L of soda and on Sunday, he sold 574 L of soda. How much soda did he sell on Saturday and Sunday?

(A) 927 liters   (B) 945 liters   (C) 978 liters   (D) 991 liters

20   A pitcher holds 956 mL of tea. A teacup holds 250 mL of tea. How much more tea does the pitcher hold than the tea cup?

(A) 618 ml   (B) 654 ml   (C) 706 ml   (D) 758 ml

Next Section: Multiply and Divide Involving Masses and Volumes

MULTIPLY AND DIVIDE INVOLVING MASSES AND VOLUMES

We can multiply and divide masses and volumes as long as the units are the same. We can multiply or divide grams with grams, kilograms with kilograms, liters with liters, and milliliters with milliliters. We cannot, for example, multiply or divide kilograms and milliliters.

When multiplying and dividing masses and volumes, we treat the values as regular numbers and complete the operation. Then, when reporting our answer, we attach the unit.

Example:

Princy purchased a 100 g package of popcorn. She wants to divide the package into 5 smaller containers so she can bring them with her lunch each day. How many grams should be in each package?

We divide 100 by 5: $100 \div 5 = 20$

Each package will contain 20 grams of popcorn.

MEASUREMENT

5.4 Multiply and Divide Involving Masses and Volumes

1 27 ml × 7 = ?

(A) 189 ml   (B) 140 ml   (C) 210 ml   (D) 235 ml

2 70 g × 10 = ?

(A) 37 grams   (B) 40 grams   (C) 48 grams   (D) 52 grams

3 88 kg ÷ 8 = ?

(A) 8 kg   (B) 11 kg   (C) 24 kg   (D) 40 kg

4 Amos has 108 L of milk and he must divide it equally into 9 containers. How many liters will be in each container?

(A) 12 L   (B) 10 L   (C) 9 L   (D) 6 L

5 Roy bought 6 slices of pizza. Each slice weighs 90 g. How many total grams of pizza did Roy buy?

(A) 500 g   (B) 520 g   (C) 540 g   (D) 560 g

6 Smith has 10 kg a cake that he must divide into 10 parts. How much weight is in each component?

(A) 2 kg   (B) 0 kg   (C) 10 kg   (D) 1 kg

7 Aaliyah bought 3 kg tomatoes and 5 kg potatoes. How many total kilograms of tomatoes and potatoes did Aaliyah buy?

(A) 12 kg   (B) 15 kg   (C) 8 kg   (D) 5 kg

8 Bella serves each of her 5 guests 70 g French fries. How many total grams of french fries did she serve?

(A) 350 g   (B) 420 g   (C) 470 g   (D) 550 g

9 Aurora has 3 bags with a mass of 90 kg. What is the mass of each bag?

(A) 10 kg   (B) 15 kg   (C) 30 kg   (D) 45 kg

10 Elvis carries 8 jugs of water and each contains 2 L. How many liters of water did she carry?

(A) 2 L   (B) 4 L   (C) 8 L   (D) 16 L

MEASUREMENT

5.4   **Multiply and Divide Involving Masses and Volumes**

11   Randy has 4 travel shampoo packets. Each shampoo contains 10 ml. How much shampoo is in each packet?

_____

12   One chocolate has a mass of 80 g. What is the mass of 6 chocolates?

_____

13   Nick makes 150 L orange juice. He divides the orange juice into 5 containers. How many liters of orange juice are in each container?

_____

14   Timothy divides the 400 ml chocolate syrup container into two smaller 40 ml containers. How many containers can he fill?

(A) 10 ml   (B) 40 ml   (C) 80 ml   (D) 100 ml

15   Zeke has 9 juice glass weights that each have a mass of 11 kg. What is the mass of all the juice glass weights?

(A) 90 kg   (B) 99 kg   (C) 20 kg   (D) 119 kg

16 A teacup has a volume of 250 ml. If a jar contains 750 ml tea, how many tea cups can it fill?

(A) 4　　　　(B) 7　　　　(C) 3　　　　(D) 5

17 Ray divides 500 g of cake into 4 equal parts. How many grams are in each part?

(A) 150 g　　(B) 100 g　　(C) 250 g　　(D) 125 g

18 A pen has a mass of 9 grams. How many pens are in a box with a mass of 81 grams? Assume the box has no mass.

(A) 11　　　　(B) 9　　　　(C) 10　　　　(D) 8

19 A bag contains 8 books. Each book weights 2 kg. What is the total weight of books in a bag?

(A) 16 kg　　(B) 8 kg　　(C) 24 kg　　(D) 2 kg

20 A water bottle has a volume of 1 L. If a bucket contains 27 L of water, how many bottles can fill?

(A) 39　　　　(B) 32　　　　(C) 27　　　　(D) 25

Next Section:
Represent and Interpret Data ≫

REPRESENT AND INTERPRET DATA

We use graphs to visually display data. We use a picture (or line) graph to display continuous data. This is data that happens over a period of time. We use a bar graph to represent one-time data (such as survey results).

Using a table of data, we can create a bar graph or a line graph, depending on the type of data. To create a bar graph, each category of the data in the table corresponds to a bar. The height or length of the bar indicates the quantity. For a line graph, we use lines to connect individual data points over a specified interval.

The following table gives the number of blocks of each color in a classroom play center.

Red	Yellow	Green	Natural
16	17	7	18

Since this data is the result of a single instance or survey, we represent it using a bar graph. The more blocks we have in a specified color, the taller our bar is. We use the left side of the graph to indicate the height of the bars and the bottom of the graph to indicate the categories.

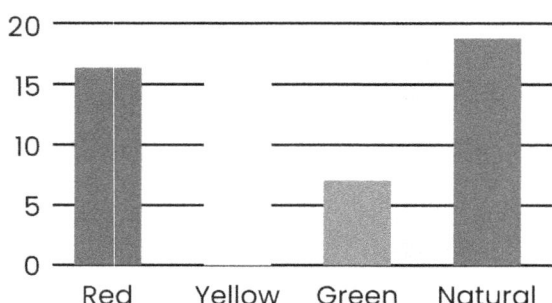

REPRESENT AND INTERPRET DATA

We can also switch the orientation of the bar graph. Instead of the bars going up from bottom to top, we can have the bars grow from left to right. With this orientation of the bar graph, the categories of blocks are given on the left side, and the quantities are depicted on the bottom. These two types of bar graphs can be used interchangeably, and neither is considered better than the other.

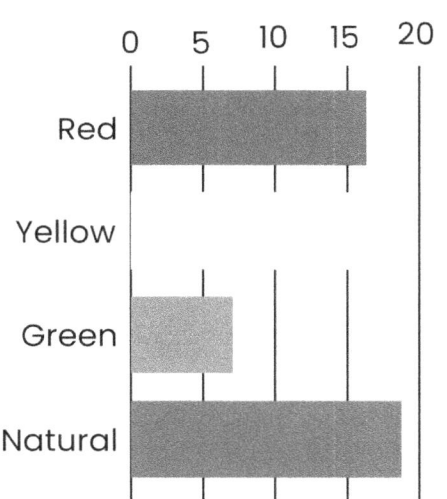

In contrast to a bar graph, a line graph is used to display data that is collected over a specified time interval. This interval can be minutes, years, or anything in between.

The following table shows the number of watermelons sold at a grocery store in an afternoon.

1:00	2:00	3:00	4:00
16	13	18	4

Since the watermelon sales data was collected over a specified time interval, we used a line graph to represent the data. We plot each data point in the table and use lines to connect the data points.

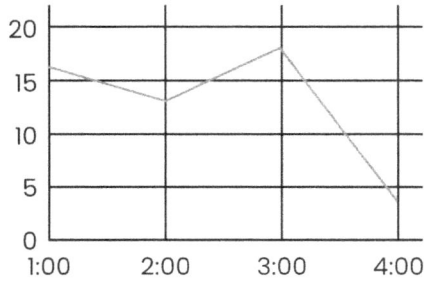

The bottom axis of the graph indicates the time interval, and the left side indicates the quantity.

5.5   Represent and Interpret Data

1   True or False: The bar graph accurately represents the table.

Domestic Animal	Quantity
Cow	56
Sheep	86
Dog	79
Cat	44

(A) True

(B) False

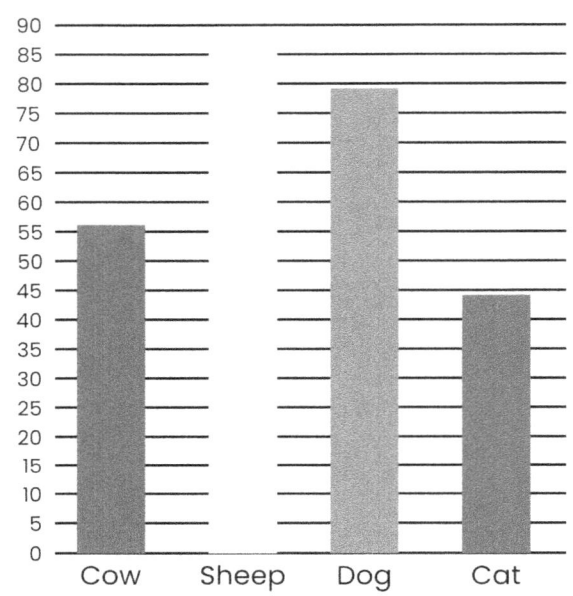

---

2   True or False: The bar graph accurately represents the table.

Birds	Quantity
Parrot	25
Eagle	10
Woodpecker	20

(A) True   (B) False

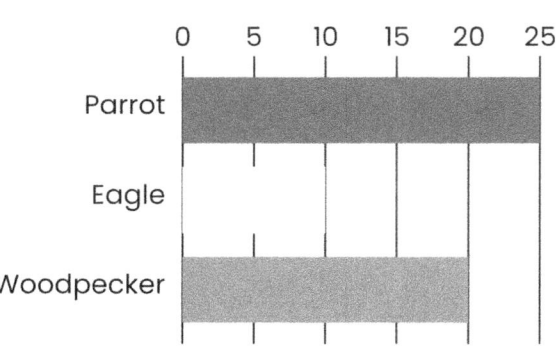

3   True or False: The line graph accurately represents the table.

Vegetables	Quantity
Pumpkin	14
Red Chili	27
Corn	11
Broccoli	17
Mushroom	35

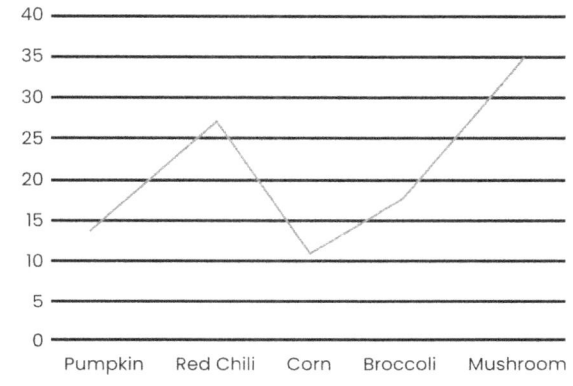

(A) True   (B) False

4   True or False: The line graph accurately represents the table.

Wild Animals	Quantity
Lion	21
Tiger	12
Zebra	9
Bear	15

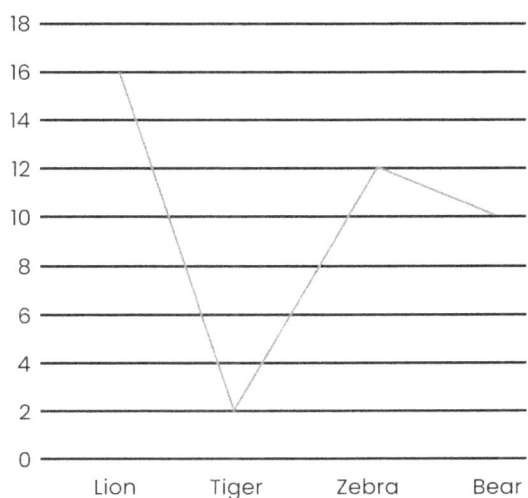

(A) True   (B) False

5.5   Represent and Interpret Data

5   Which table is depicted by the bar graph?

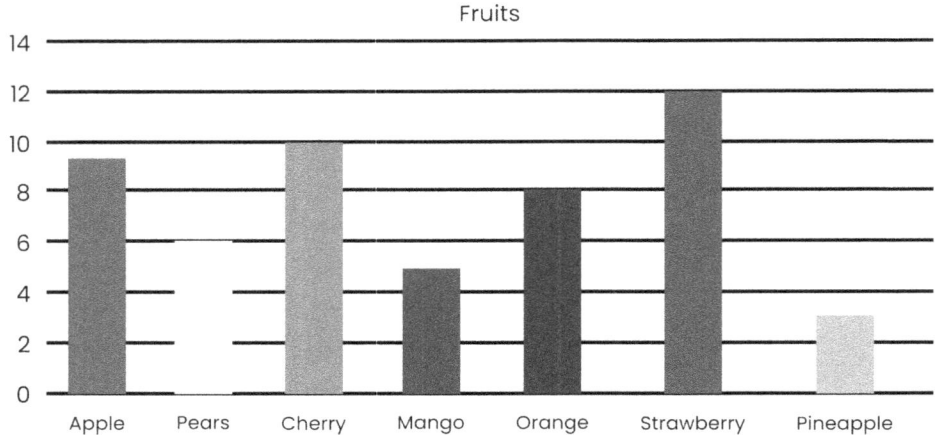

A

Apple	11
Pears	5
Cherry	2
Mango	9
Orange	12
Strawberry	5
Pineapple	13

B

Apple	1
Pears	3
Cherry	5
Mango	7
Orange	9
Strawberry	11
Pineapple	13

C

Apple	9
Pears	6
Cherry	10
Mango	5
Orange	8
Strawberry	12
Pineapple	3

D

Apple	2
Pears	4
Cherry	6
Mango	8
Orange	10
Strawberry	12
Pineapple	3

6 True or False: The line graph accurately represents the table.

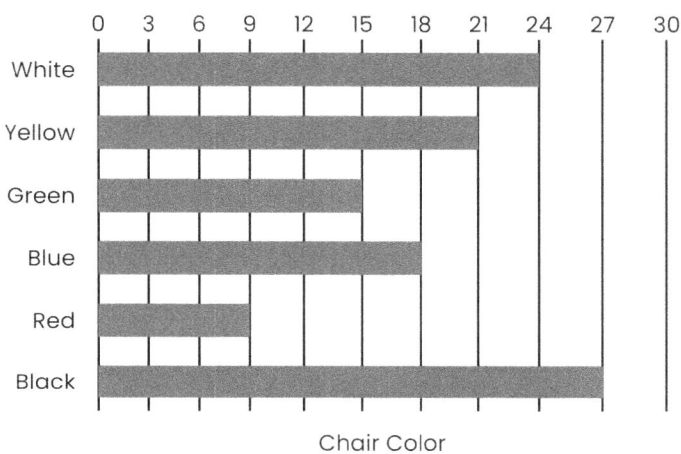

Chair Color

(A)

Black	20
Red	17
Blue	11
Green	18
Yellow	9
White	25

(B)

Black	17
Red	15
Blue	8
Green	16
Yellow	6
White	23

(C)

Black	12
Red	10
Blue	13
Green	21
Yellow	1
White	18

(D)

Black	27
Red	9
Blue	18
Green	15
Yellow	21
White	24

5.5   **Represent and Interpret Data**

7   Which table is depicted by the bar graph?

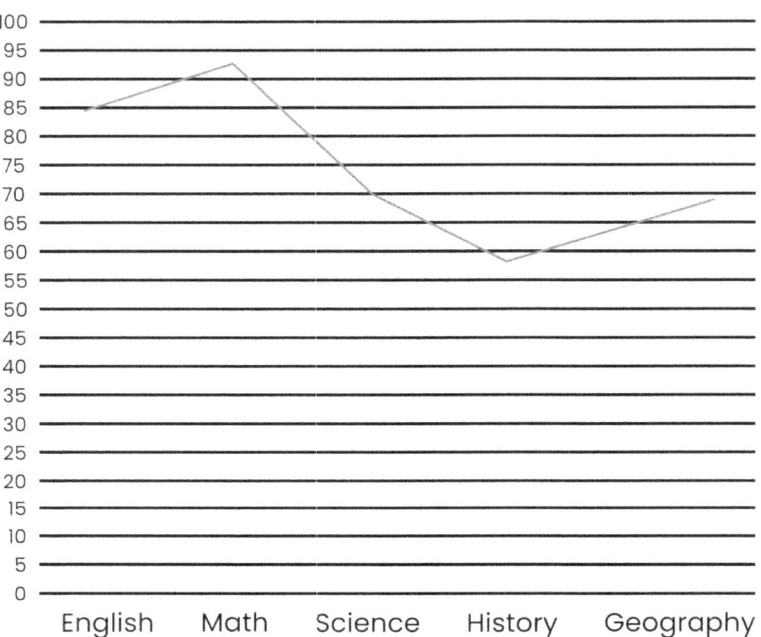

A

English	85
Math	92
Science	70
History	58
Geography	69

B

English	80
Math	85
Science	65
History	51
Geography	60

C

English	67
Math	58
Science	62
History	90
Geography	80

D

English	90
Math	100
Science	98
History	95
Geography	97

8 Which table is depicted by the line graph?

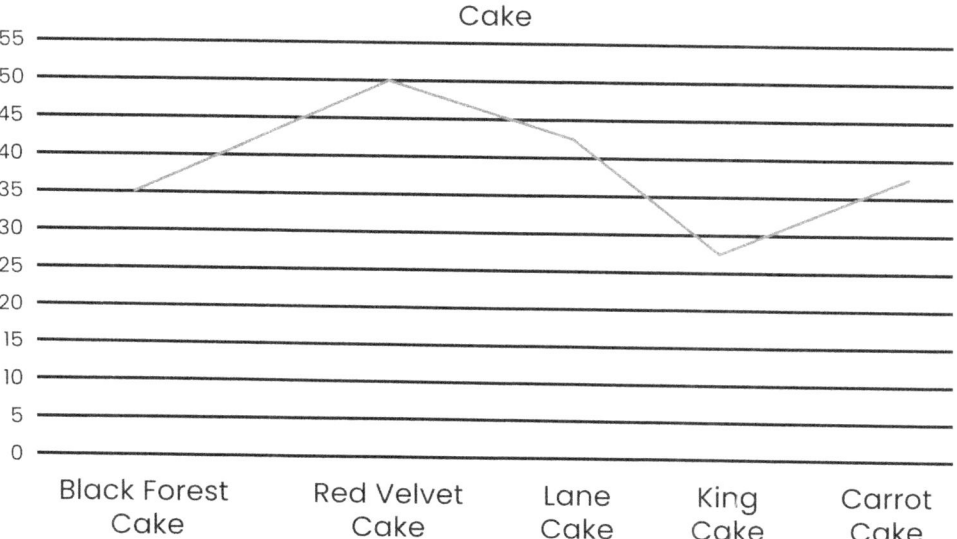

A

Black Forest Cake	15
Red Velvet Cake	34
Lane Cake	49
King Cake	36
Carrot Cake	21

B

Black Forest Cake	50
Red Velvet Cake	40
Lane Cake	30
King Cake	20
Carrot Cake	10

C

Black Forest Cake	35
Red Velvet Cake	50
Lane Cake	42
King Cake	26
Carrot Cake	38

D

Black Forest Cake	35
Red Velvet Cake	28
Lane Cake	40
King Cake	30
Carrot Cake	45

5.5 Represent and Interpret Data

9 Use the graph to answer the question.
How many people like Hot dogs?

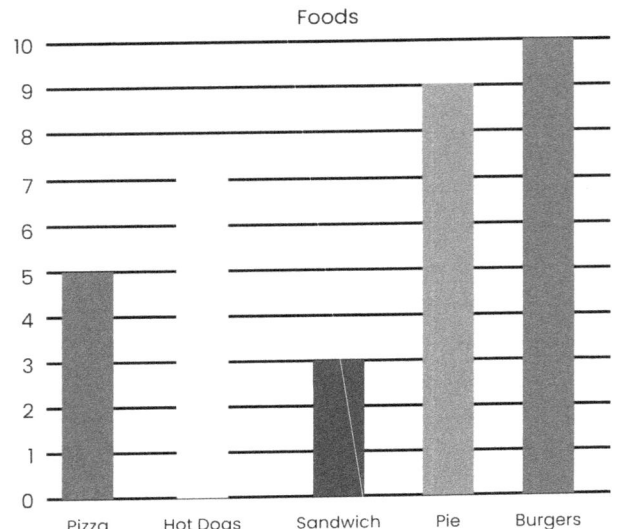

A) 3

B) 7

C) 5

D) 9

10 Use the graph to answer the question. How many more mulberry trees are there in the garden than plum trees?

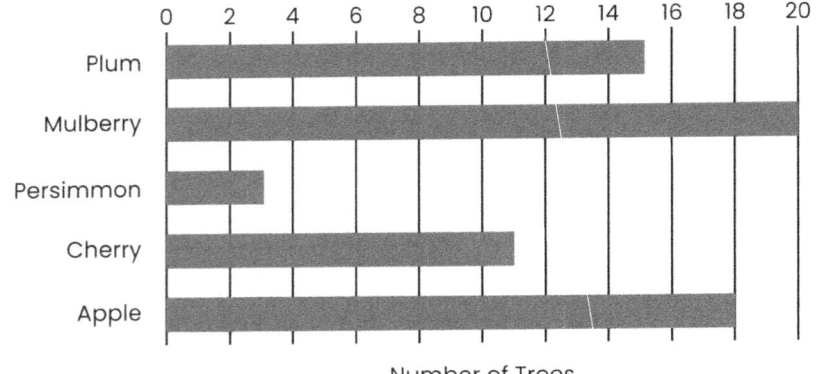

Number of Trees

A) 20

B) 3

C) 15

D) 5

11 Use the graph to answer the question. How many Almond joy and Butterfinger does the store have?

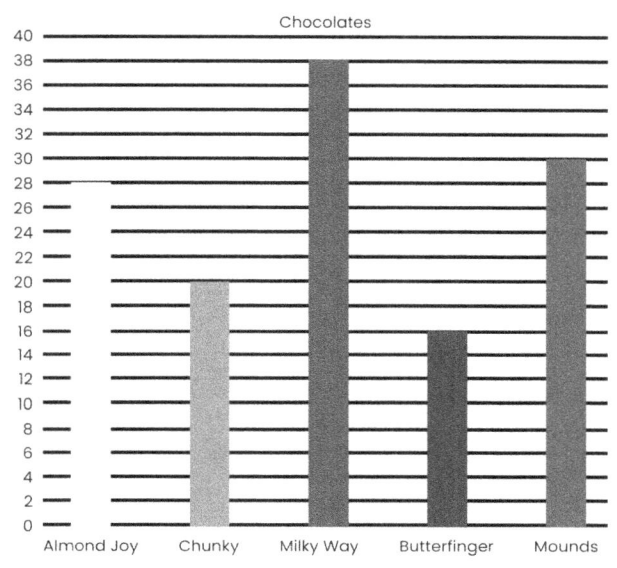

(A) 44

(B) 36

(C) 38

(D) 18

12 Adam bought all the crayons and one-fourth of the pens. How many crayons and pens does Adam buy combined?

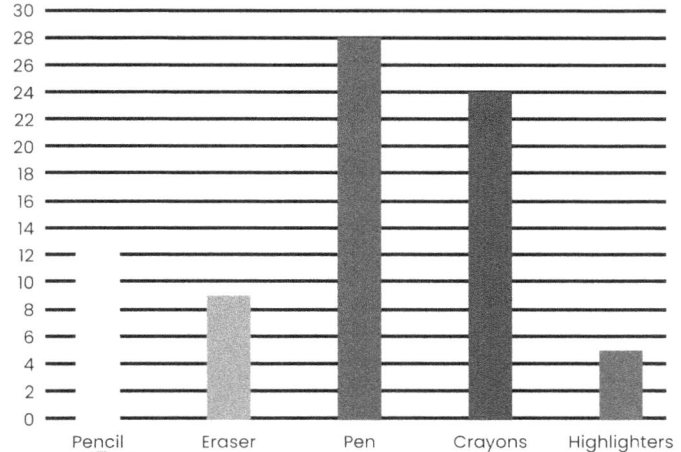

(A) 23

(B) 39

(C) 31

(D) 28

5.5   **Represent and Interpret Data**

13   Ariel bought all the shirts, skirts, and T-shirts. How many total pieces of clothing Ariel buys?

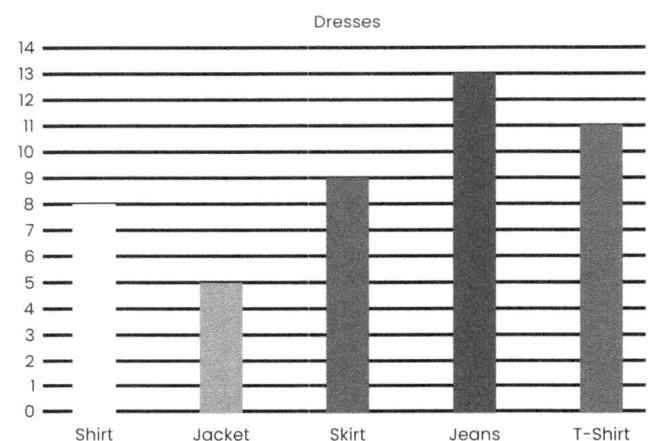

Dresses

- (A) 13
- (B) 28
- (C) 37
- (D) 41

14   What is the length of the rectangle?

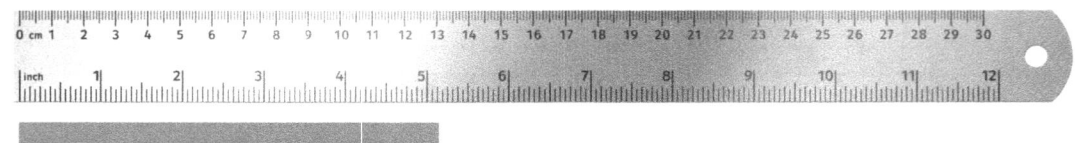

- (A) $5\frac{1}{2}$ inches
- (B) 5 inches
- (C) $5\frac{1}{4}$ inches
- (D) $5\frac{3}{4}$ inches

Represent and Interpret Data   5.5

15 What is the length of the rectangle?

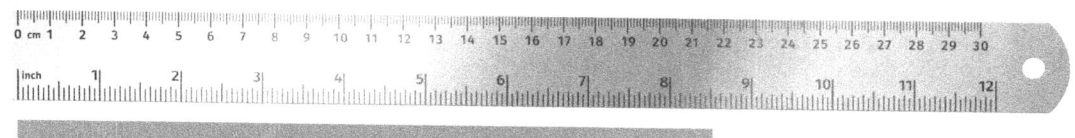

(A) $7\frac{1}{2}$ inches   (B) $8\frac{1}{2}$ inches   (C) $8\frac{1}{4}$ inches   (D) $9\frac{3}{4}$ inches

16 What is the distance between the lion and the tiger?

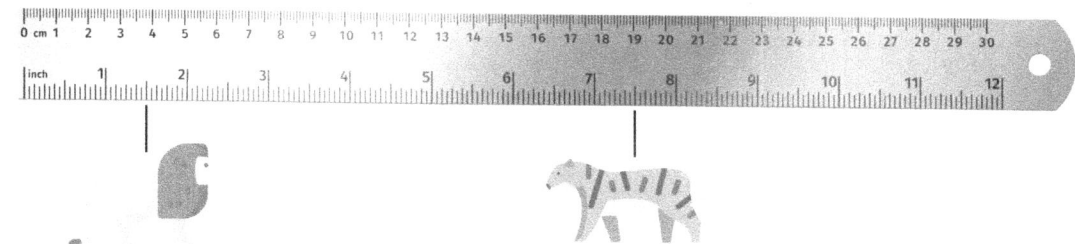

(A) $7\frac{1}{2}$ inches   (B) $8\frac{1}{2}$ inches   (C) $8\frac{1}{4}$ inches   (D) 6 inches

MEASUREMENT

5.5 Represent and Interpret Data

17 What is the distance between the dog and the cat?

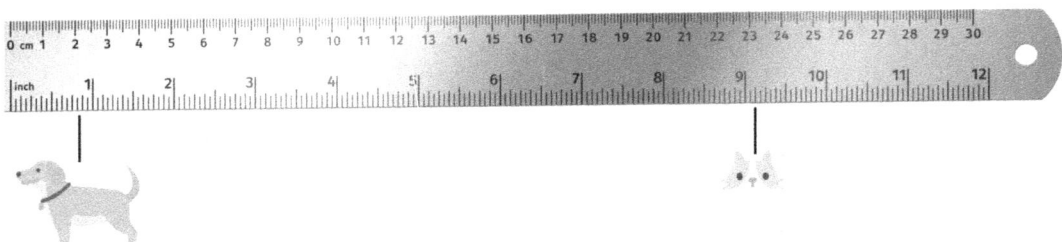

(A) $8\frac{1}{2}$ inches (B) $8\frac{1}{4}$ inches (C) $8\frac{3}{4}$ inches (D) $9\frac{1}{4}$ inches

18 How far is the car from the tree?

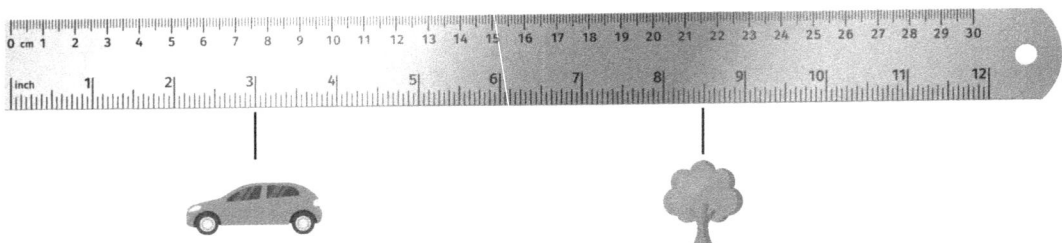

19   What is the distance between the fish and the cow?

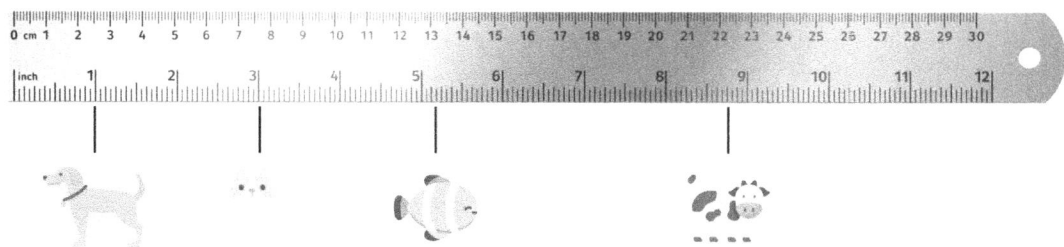

_____

20   How far are the cherries from the tree?

_____

Next Section: Chapter Review ▶▶

5.6   Chapter Review

1   Which is a better unit to use to describe the volume of a bottle of lavender essential oil?

(A) Liters   (B) Milliliters   (C) Grams   (D) Kilograms

2   What is the length of the cylinder?

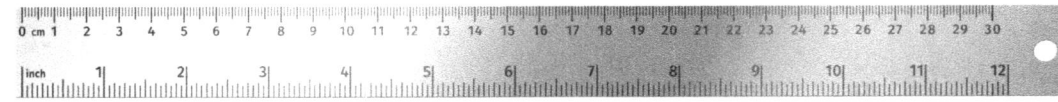

(A) 5 inches   (B) $4\frac{1}{4}$ inches   (C) 5 inches   (D) $3\frac{3}{4}$ inches

3   What time does the clock show?

(A) Eight forty   (B) Twelve nine

(C) Nine forty   (D) Seven forty-seven

4 State whether this is true or false. The sofa has a length of $6\frac{1}{2}$ inches?

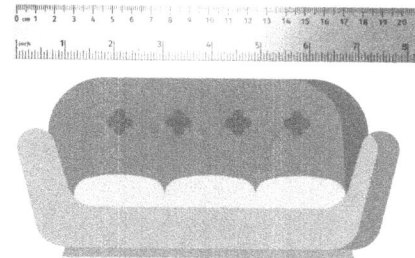

(A) True

(B) False

5 Which is a better unit to describe the mass of the men's running shoes?

(A) Liters   (B) Milliliters   (C) Grams   (D) Kilograms

6 State True or False. The image of the line segment is $5\frac{1}{4}$ inches?

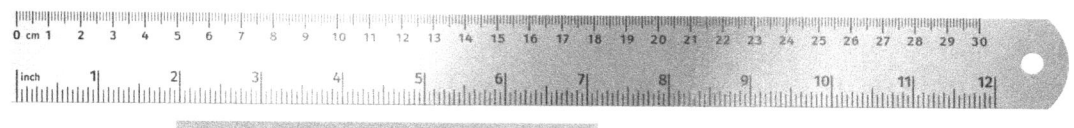

(A) True   (B) False

163

5.6   Chapter Review

7   Which digital clock shows the same time as this analog clock?

(A)  03:23

(B)  04:16

(C)  01:43

(D) 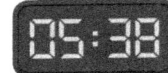 05:38

8   What is 8:17 + 3:53 = ?

_____

9   Zachary studies for 2 hours 20 minutes. If he starts to study at 4:35, what time is he finished studying?

_____

10   Tess finishes shopping in 4 hours, 47 minutes. She finished shopping at 7:54. At what time did she begin shopping?

_____

11 Jason cooks 403 grams of fish. He then cooks 312 grams of fish more. How many grams of fish did he cook in total?

A) 715 g   B) 793 g   C) 701 g   D) 726 g

12 Liam buys 749 L of milk. If he uses 299 L, how many liters of milk are left?

A) 649 L   B) 579 L   C) 450 L   D) 390 L

13 What is 8 ml × 9 = ?

A) 81 ml   B) 72 ml   C) 76 ml   D) 68 ml

14 Neil is carrying 7 pineapples that each have a mass of 2 kg. What is the total mass of the pineapples he is carrying?

A) 7 kg   B) 9 kg   C) 11 kg   D) 14 kg

5.6   Chapter Review

15 Mary has 93 colored pencils. He divides the colored pencils into 3 and gives them to her 3 children. How many colored pencils does she give to each of her children?

(A) 29   (B) 31   (C) 36   (D) 32

16 Select the analog clock that displays the same time as the timeline.

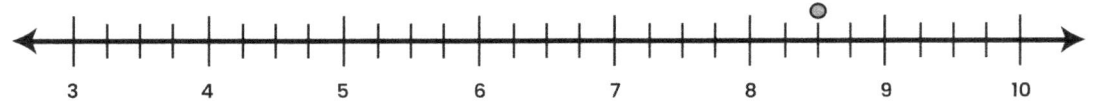

(A)    (B)    (C)    (D)

17 Determine the amount of time that has elapsed.
Start: 5:39, Stop: 10:43.

(A) 5:04   (B) 5:26   (C) 6:01   (D) 5:16

18   True or False: The line graph accurately represents the table.

Grade	No of Student
1	20
3	45
5	35
7	40

(A) True

(B) False

19   Use the graph to answer the question. How many more black color shoes than blue color shoes?

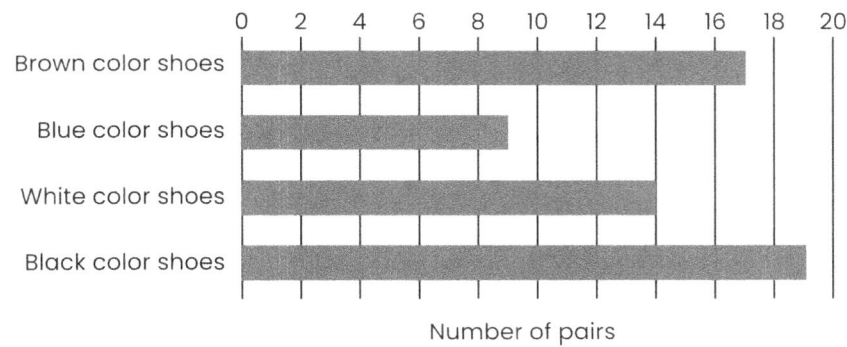

Number of pairs

(A) 28   (B) 19   (C) 9   (D) 10

5.6   **Chapter Review**

20   What is the distance between the watermelon and the banana?

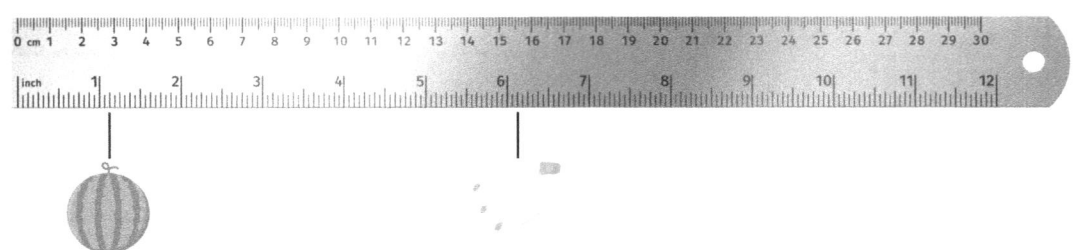

(A) $5\frac{1}{4}$ inches   (B) 5 inches   (C) $6\frac{1}{4}$ inches   (D) 6 inches

Next Chapter:
Geometric Measurement

CHAPTER 6

GEOMETRIC MEASUREMENT

COMPLETE THE PATTERN

 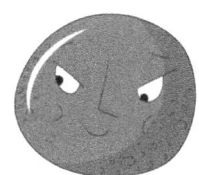 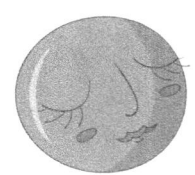 

   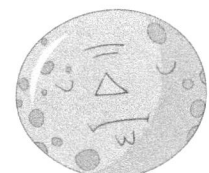

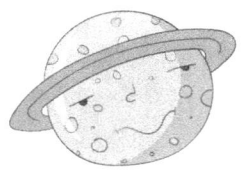   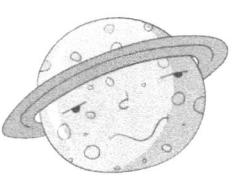

AREA OF SQUARES, RECTANGLES, AND RECTILINEAR FIGURES

Area of Square:

A plane figure is a two-dimensional figure. The area of a plane figure is the size of the surface. We can measure area in terms of square units or unit squares. A unit square is a square with a side length of 1 and therefore, is said to have one square unit of area. To find the area of a two-dimensional figure using unit squares, we count the unit squares. Since each unit square has an area of 1, we find the area by counting.

Example:

Each of the squares in the figure is a unit square. What is the area of the white shape?

We can find the area of the white shape by counting the number of white squares in the figure. When we count, we determine there are 31 white unit squares. This means that the white shape in the figure has an area of 31.

Area of Rectangle:

A unit square is a 1 unit by 1 unit square with an area of 1 square unit. We can count the number of unit squares in a rectangle to determine the area of a rectangle. If we know the dimensions of a rectangle, we can draw the appropriate number of unit squares and count them to find the area.

AREA OF SQUARES, RECTANGLES, AND RECTILINEAR FIGURES

Area of Rectilinear:

Up until this point, we have been tasked only with finding the area of a square or a rectangle. However, we can use these skills to find the area of more complicated figures by decomposing them into squares and rectangles. Remember that if we have a square or a rectangle, we can find the area by multiplying the length times the width, or tiling the shape and counting the unit squares.

Let's use an example to understand how we can decompose a more complex shape into rectangles or squares to find the area.

The figure below is complex and therefore, we cannot simply multiply the values of the two sides and find the area. Instead, we must decompose the figure into rectangles and find the area of each rectangle. Then we add the areas of each rectangle to obtain the area of the entire figure.

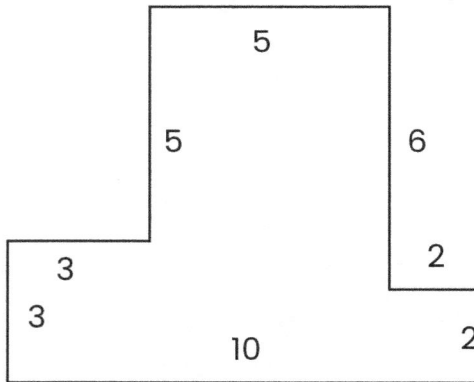

Example:

A rectangle has 2 rows and 4 columns. How many unit squares are in the rectangle?

To solve this problem, we first draw a rectangular table with 2 rows and 4 columns where each of the squares is of equal size.

AREA OF SQUARES, RECTANGLES, AND RECTILINEAR FIGURES

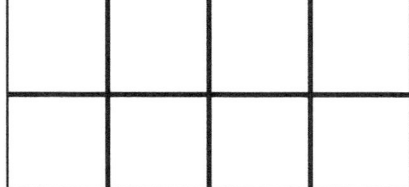

Then, we count the number of unit squares in the rectangle. The total number of unit squares is the area. Therefore, the area of a rectangle with 2 rows and 4 columns is 8.

If we are given the dimensions of a rectangle, we can draw the appropriate number of unit squares in the rectangle and then count the unit squares to obtain the area. We can also use multiplication to check our work.

6.1 Area of Squares, Rectangles, and Rectilinear Figures

1 A rectangle has 3 rows and 3 columns. How many squares are in the rectangle?

A) 6   B) 9   C) 4   D) 12

2 A rectangle has 5 rows and 6 columns. How many squares are in the rectangle?

A) 36   B) 39   C) 40   D) 30

3 What is the area of the rectangle?

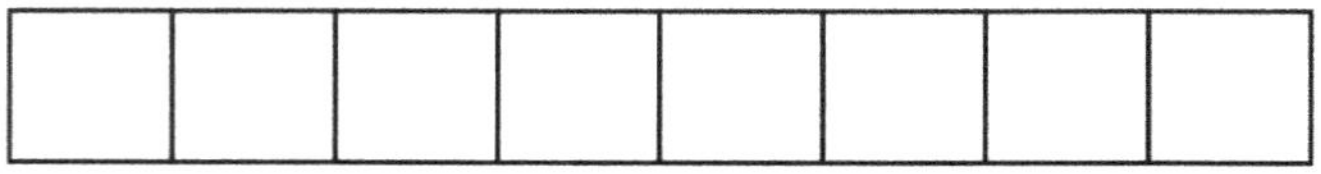

A) 8   B) 9   C) 4   D) 12

4 Find the area of the rectangle by drawing columns and rows of one unit square to form a grid.

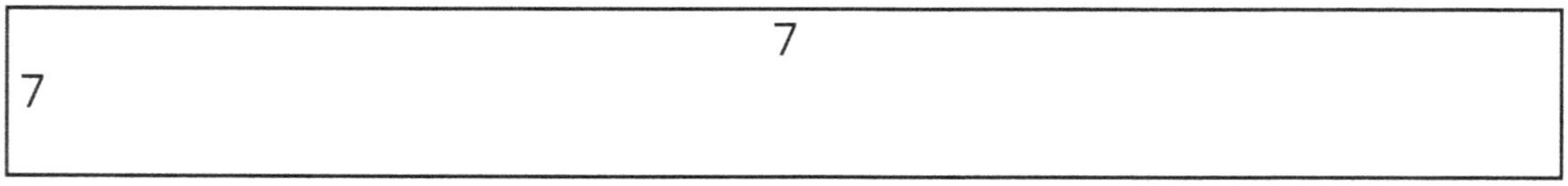

7

7

A) 36   B) 49   C) 40   D) 55

Area of Squares, Rectangles, and Rectilinear Figures

6.1

5 A rectangle has 1 row and 5 columns. What is the area of the rectangle?

Ⓐ 8 Ⓑ 9 Ⓒ 5 Ⓓ 3

6 What is the missing number in the distributive property equation for the area of the rectangle? $7 \times (3 + \underline{\quad}) = 42$.

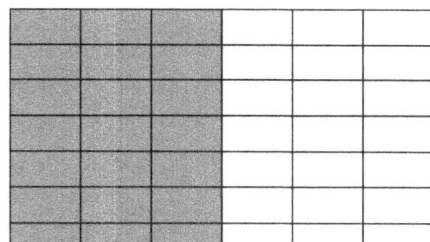

Ⓐ 3
Ⓑ 4
Ⓒ 5
Ⓓ 2

7 What is the missing number in the distributive property equation for the area of the rectangle? $\underline{\quad} \times (3 + 1) = 12$.

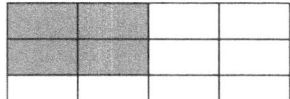

Ⓐ 3 Ⓑ 4
Ⓒ 5 Ⓓ 2

8 Without counting each individual unit square, what is the area of the rectangle?

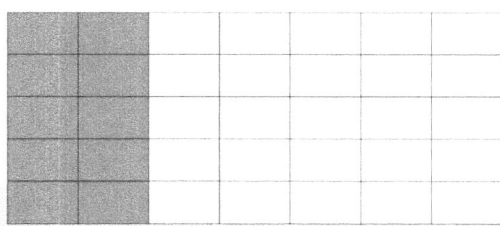

Ⓐ 30 Ⓑ 40
Ⓒ 50 Ⓓ 25

6.1   Area of Squares, Rectangles, and
Rectilinear Figures

---

9   Two books are laid side by side. The books have the same length of 9 inches. The book 1 is 7 inches wide, and Book 2 is 6 inches wide. What is the area of both books when they are laid side by side?

_____

10   A restaurant pushes two tables together for a large party. The first table is 10 feet wide and 11 feet long. The second table is 15 feet wide and 11 feet long. What is the area of both tables pushed together?

_____

11   A construction worker must cut a rectangle out of a tile to make room for an outlet. The original tile measures 6 inches by 5 inches. The construction worker cuts an inch by 2 inch piece out of the tile. What is the area of the remaining piece of tile?

_____

12   A computer measures 8 inches by 10 inches. When the CD drive is open, it measures 4 inches by 5 inches. What is the area of a computer when the CD drive is open?

_____

13 A piece of laminate flooring measures 30 inches by 9 inches. An installer must cut a 5 inch by 12 inch section out of the corner of the board so it will fit in a doorway. What is the area of the remaining piece of flooring?

_____

14 To construct a paper boat, Chris cuts equal-sized squares out of the corners of her paper. She begins with a 15-inch by 17-inch sheet of paper and cuts 4-inch squares out of each corner. What is the area of the remaining paper?

_____

15 A gardener is designing a new raised garden bed. The bed will be V-shaped. The bottom of the V will be a rectangle measuring 4 feet by 8 feet. Each of the sides of the V will be a rectangle measuring 3 feet by 9 feet. What is the total area of the garden bed?

_____

6.1 Area of Squares, Rectangles, and Rectilinear Figures

16 The following shape is made of unit squares. Determine the area of the shape.

A) 2 B) 3

C) 4 D) 5

17 What is the area of the rectilinear figure?

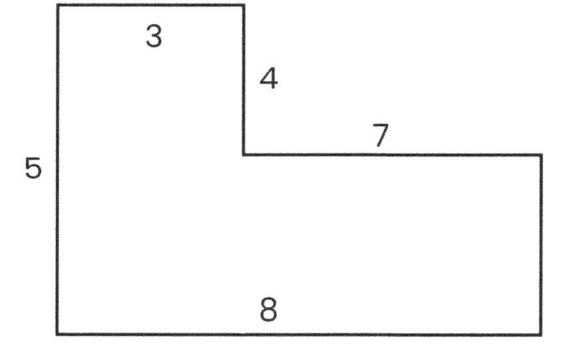

A) 28

B) 32

C) 45

D) 50

18 An outlet cover is a rectangular piece of plastic with a small rectangle cut out of it. The outer dimensions of the outlet cover are 4 inches by 6 inches. The dimensions of the hole cut into the cover are 2 inches by 3 inches. What is the area that the outlet covers?

A) 28 B) 18 C) 15 D) 10

19 The following shape is made of unit squares. Determine the area of the shape.

(A) 20   (B) 18

(C) 15   (D) 12

20 A rectangle has 5 rows and 9 columns. How many squares are in the rectangle?

(A) 50   (B) 45   (C) 40   (D) 30

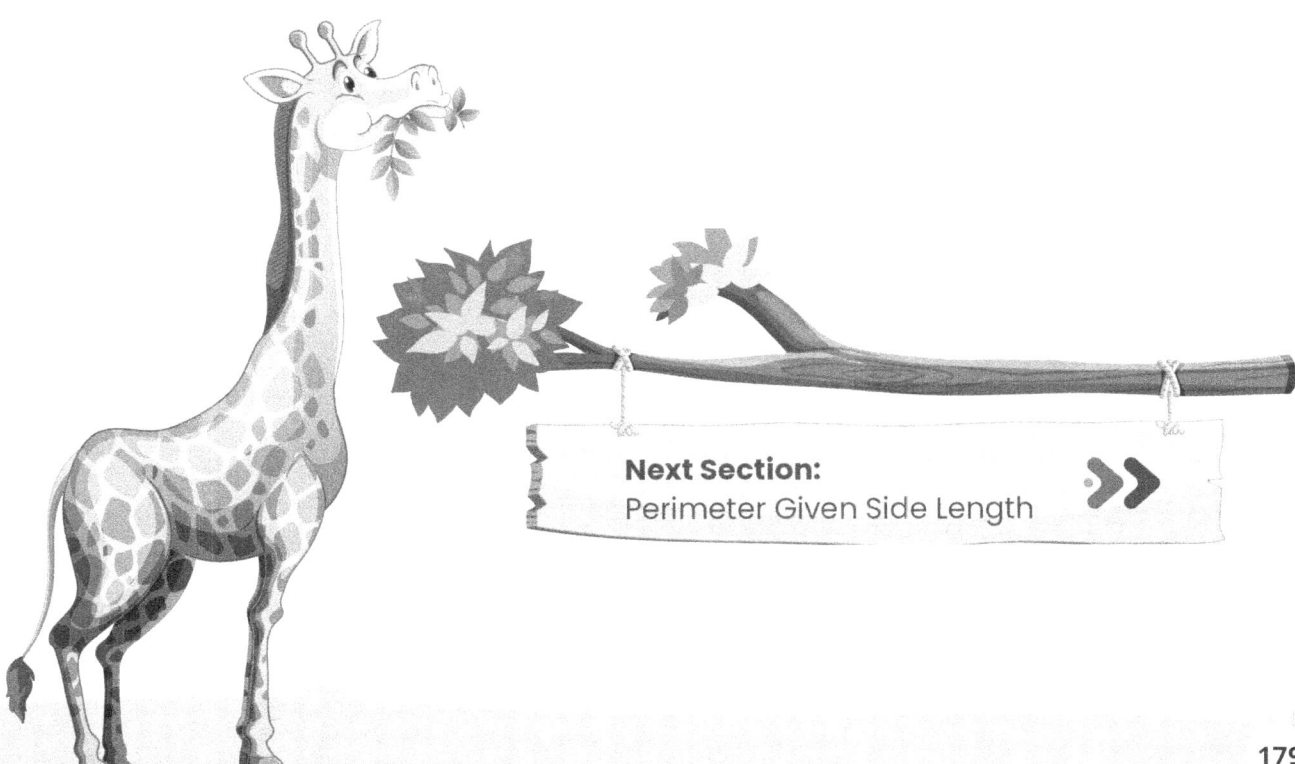

Next Section:
Perimeter Given Side Length ≫

179

PERIMETER GIVEN SIDE LENGTH

The perimeter is the distance around a figure or shape. To find the perimeter of a shape, we add the length of all sides.

Example:

Find the perimeter of the shape.

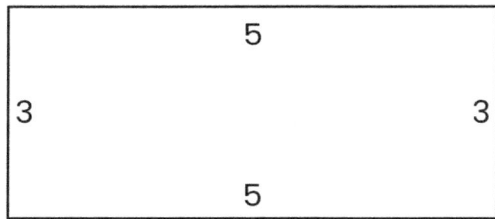

We know that the lengths of the sides of the shape are 5, 5, 3 and 3. To find the perimeter, we add all of these values together.

$$5 + 5 + 3 + 3 = 10 + 6 = 16$$

The perimeter of the shape is 16.

1   What is the perimeter of the figure?

36

25

(A) 100   (B) 145

(C) 122   (D) 130

2   What is the perimeter of the figure?

89

55

(A) 128   (B) 145

(C) 200   (D) 288

3   What is the perimeter of the figure?

63

17

(A) 128   (B) 145

(C) 160   (D) 190

4   What is the perimeter of the figure?

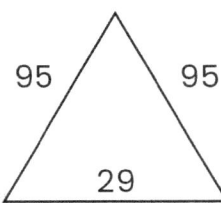

95   95

29

(A) 219   (B) 211

(C) 230   (D) 200

181

6.2 **Perimeter Given Side Length**

5 What is the perimeter of the figure?

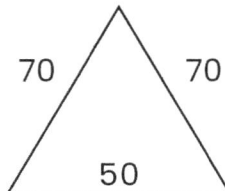

A) 190   B) 211

C) 230   D) 200

6 What is the perimeter of the figure?

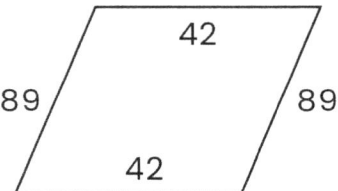

A) 190   B) 262

C) 230   D) 290

7 What is the perimeter of the figure?

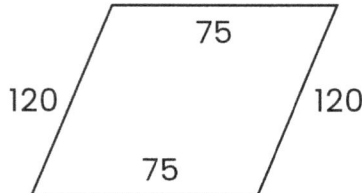

A) 390   B) 250

C) 350   D) 450

8 A 5-sided figure has lengths of 30, 71, 48, 80 and 25 feet. What is the perimeter of the figure?

A) 260   B) 254   C) 200   D) 290

9 A common floor tile is a 20-inch square. What is the perimeter of such a tile?

(A) 120   (B) 100   (C) 80   (D) 180

10 A twin mattress is 69 inches wide and 95 inches long. What is the perimeter of the mattress?

(A) 320   (B) 328   (C) 315   (D) 290

11 A large area rug is rectangular. It is 15 feet wide and 22 feet long. What is the perimeter of the rugs?

(A) 74   (B) 80   (C) 69   (D) 90

12 What is the perimeter of the figure?

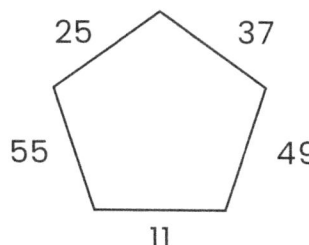

25   37

55   49

11

(A) 174   (B) 180

(C) 169   (D) 177

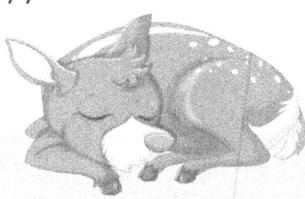

6.2   Perimeter Given Side Length

13   What is the perimeter of the figure?

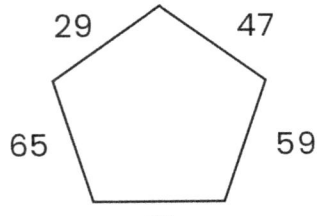

A) 231   B) 240

C) 259   D) 297

14   A horse corral is a six-sided figure. The lengths of the sides are 39, 46, 52, 11, 71, and 30 feet. What is the perimeter of the horse corral?

A) 231   B) 249   C) 259   D) 297

15   A piece of land is shaped like a triangle. The legs of the triangle are the same length at 750 feet, and the base of the triangle is 890 feet. What is the perimeter of the piece of land?

A) 2391   B) 2490   C) 2590   D) 2390

16   When drawn on a map, the road trip a family took is in the shape of a triangle. The first leg of the trip was 390 miles. The second leg of the trip was 469 miles. The final leg of the trip was 743 miles. What is the total perimeter of the triangle created by the legs of the road trip?

A) 2391   B) 2490   C) 2590   D) 2390

17   A 5-sided figure has sides of length 77, 52, 40, 33, and 64. What is the perimeter of the figure?

(A) 266   (B) 249   (C) 259   (D) 297

18   A farmer is building a new barn. The barn will be rectangular in shape with a length of 90 feet and a width of 52 feet. What is the perimeter of the barn?

(A) 286   (B) 279   (C) 284   (D) 297

19   A movie theatre screen is rectangular in shape. If a particular screen is 57 feet wide and 40 feet tall, what is the perimeter of the screen?

(A) 186   (B) 179   (C) 284   (D) 194

20   The lengths of the sides of a 4-sided figure are 29 cm, 82 cm, 31 cm, and 95 cm. What is the perimeter of the figure?

(A) 237   (B) 179   (C) 284   (D) 194

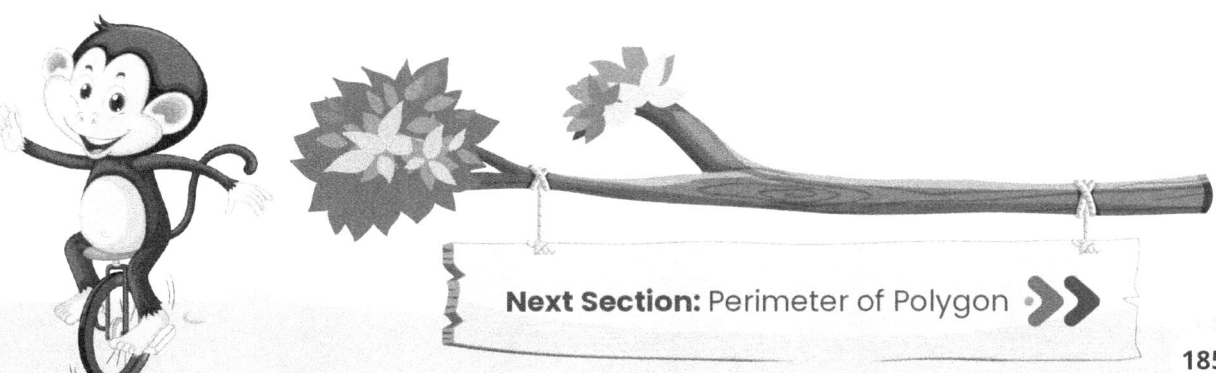

Next Section: Perimeter of Polygon ❯❯

PERIMETER OF POLYGON

The perimeter of a polygon is defined as the total distance around the outside of the shape. We find the perimeter of a figure by adding the length of the sides.

Example:

Find the perimeter of the polygon.

```
               20
   ┌──────────────────────┐
   │                      │
12 │                      │ 12
   │          20          │
   └──────────────────────┘
```

First, we formulate our addition problem, making sure to include the length of each side of the figure.

$$12 + 20 + 12 + 20$$

Then, we add the lengths of the sides together.

$$12 + 20 + 12 + 20 = 10 + 2 + 20 + 10 + 2 + 20 = 60 + 4 = 64$$

The perimeter of the polygon is 64.

1 Robert drew an equilateral triangle (all the sides are the same length). If the length of a side is 155 cm, What is the perimeter of the triangle?

(A) 485   (B) 465   (C) 500   (D) 525

2 Three streets in a neighborhood join to form a triangle. The length of the first street is 175 yards. The length of the second street is 148 yards. The length of the third street is 205 yards. What is the perimeter of the triangle formed by the three streets?

(A) 485   (B) 555   (C) 500   (D) 528

3 What is the perimeter of an equilateral heptagon with a side length of 99 inches?

(A) 693   (B) 655   (C) 625   (D) 700

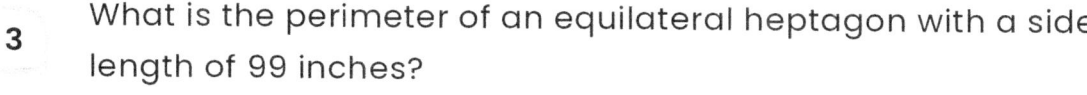

4 A given hexagon has 3 sets of matching sides. The length of the first set is 57 cm. The length of the second set is 39 cm. The length of the third set is 78 cm. What is the perimeter of the hexagon?

(A) 428   (B) 320   (C) 368   (D) 348

6.3　　**Perimeter of Polygon**

5　A fireplace is rectangular and reaches all the way to the ceiling of a house. If the width of the fireplace is 15 feet and the length of the fireplace is 32 feet, what is the perimeter of the fireplace?

(A) 104　　　(B) 94　　　(C) 84　　　(D) 74

6　A dodecagon is a 12-sided polygon. If the sides of a dodecagon are equal in length at 85 inches, what is the perimeter of the dodecagon?

(A) 1040　　　(B) 940　　　(C) 1020　　　(D) 1060

7　What is the perimeter of the figure?

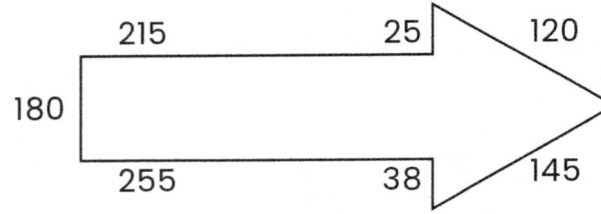

(A) 978　　(B) 940

(C) 1020　　(D) 1060

8　What is the perimeter of the figure?

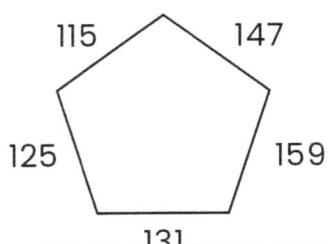

(A) 778　　(B) 677

(C) 650　　(D) 627

9 What is the perimeter of the figure?

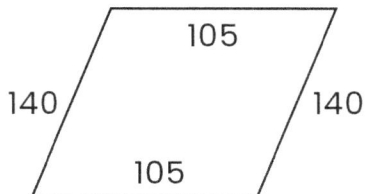

(A) 570   (B) 690

(C) 490   (D) 627

10 A kitchen towel is rectangular in shape. The width of the towel is 250 inches, and the length is 82 inches. What is the perimeter of the towel?

(A) 664   (B) 690   (C) 564   (D) 627

11 A square has a perimeter of 60 inches. What is the length of one side of the square?

(A) 15   (B) 10   (C) 20   (D) 25

12 A square has a perimeter of 16 yards. What is the length of one side of the square?

(A) 5   (B) 4   (C) 3   (D) 9

6.3   Perimeter of Polygon

13 A rectangle has a perimeter of 430 mm. The lengths of the 3 sides of the rectangle are 135 mm, 135 mm, and 80 mm. What is the length of the missing side?

(A) 85   (B) 80   (C) 135   (D) 90

14 A trapezoid is a 4-sided figure with a top, bottom, and two equal sides. The perimeter of a trapezoid is 360 mm. The lengths of the 3 sides of the trapezoid are 55 mm, 125 mm, and 125 mm. What is the length of the missing side?

(A) 55   (B) 60   (C) 125   (D) 110

15 An equilateral octagon has a perimeter of 128 mm. What is the length of one side of the octagon?

(A) 11   (B) 14   (C) 16   (D) 19

16 An equilateral decagon has a perimeter of 270 inches. What is the length of one side of the decagon?

(A) 25   (B) 24   (C) 27   (D) 30

17 An equilateral pentagon has 5 equal sides. If the perimeter of an equilateral pentagon is 115 mm, what is the length of one side?

(A) 23 (B) 24 (C) 27 (D) 30

18 A rectangle has a perimeter of 315 cm. The lengths of 3 sides of the rectangle are 65 cm, 90 cm, and 95 cm. What is the length of the missing side?

(A) 63 (B) 90 (C) 95 (D) 65

19 A square has a perimeter of 180 cm. What is the length of one side of the square?

(A) 33 (B) 40 (C) 45 (D) 55

20 An equilateral triangle has a perimeter of 225 mm. What is the length of one side of the triangle?

(A) 72 (B) 75 (C) 85 (D) 79

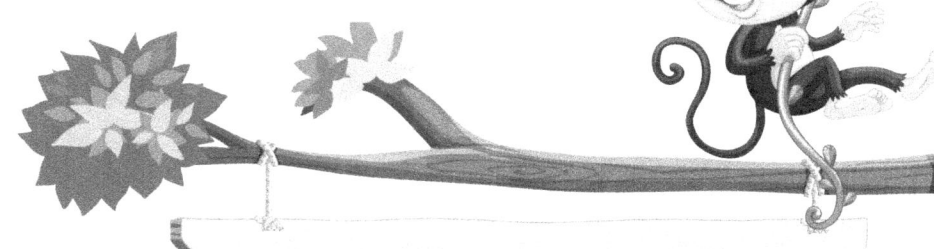

Next Section: Rectangles With The Perimeter and Areas

A rectangle is a 2-dimensional shape with four sides, where opposite sides are equal in length and all angles are right angles.The perimeter of a rectangle is the distance around the outside of the shape, which is the sum of the lengths of all four sides.The area of a rectangle is the amount of space inside the shape. To find the area of a rectangle, you can multiply the length and width together.

Shapes can have the same area, but a different perimeter. For example, the figures below have the same area, but different perimeters.

$$\begin{array}{|c|} \hline 6 \\ \qquad\qquad 2 \\ \\ \hline \end{array}$$

Area: 6 × 2 = 12.

Perimeter: 6 + 6 + 2 + 2 = 16.

1 A rectangle has a width of 2 inches and a length of 8 inches. What is the area of the rectangle?

(A) 12   (B) 15   (C) 16   (D) 20

2 A rectangle has a width of 2 inches and a length of 8 inches. What is the perimeter of the rectangle?

(A) 22   (B) 25   (C) 16   (D) 20

3 A rectangle has a length of 12 inches and a length of 22 inches. What is the area of the rectangle?

(A) 222   (B) 250   (C) 264   (D) 234

4 A rectangle has a length of 12 inches and a length of 22 inches. What is the perimeter of the rectangle?

(A) 22   (B) 50   (C) 68   (D) 35

6.4 **Rectangles With The Perimeter and Areas**

5 A rectangle has a width of 5 inches and a length of 15 inches. Select the dimension of the rectangle that has the same area.

(A) A rectangle with a length of 2 inches and a width of 8 inches.

(B) A rectangle with a length of 3 inches and a width of 5 inches.

(C) A rectangle with a length of 10 inches and a width of 5 inches.

(D) A rectangle with a length of 25 inches and a width of 3 inches.

6 A rectangle has a width of 3 inches and a length of 66 inches. Select the dimension of the rectangle that has the same area.

(A) A rectangle with a length of 33 inches and a width of 6 inches.

(B) A rectangle with a length of 30 inches and a width of 5 inches.

(C) A rectangle with a length of 10 inches and a width of 5 inches.

(D) A rectangle with a length of 25 inches and a width of 3 inches.

7 A rectangle with a width of 5 inches and a length of 14 inches. Select the dimension of the rectangle with the same perimeter.

(A) A rectangle with a length of 6 inches and a width of 12 inches.

(B) A rectangle with a length of 8 inches and a width of 5 inches.

(C) A rectangle with a length of 10 inches and a width of 9 inches.

(D) A rectangle with a length of 15 inches and a width of 9 inches.

8 A rectangle with a width of 6 inches and a length of 12 inches.
Select the dimension of the rectangle with the same perimeter.

(A) A rectangle with a length of 8 inches and a width of 16 inches.

(B) A rectangle with a length of 15 inches and a width of 3 inches.

(C) A rectangle with a length of 10 inches and a width of 9 inches.

(D) A rectangle with a length of 15 inches and a width of 9 inches.

9 A rectangle with a width of 16 inches and a length of 30 inches.
Select the dimension of the rectangle with the same perimeter.

(A) A rectangle with a length of 18 inches and a width of 26 inches.

(B) A rectangle with a length of 22 inches and a width of 24 inches.

(C) A rectangle with a length of 10 inches and a width of 19 inches.

(D) A rectangle with a length of 25 inches and a width of 9 inches.

10 A rectangle has a width of 15 inches and a length of 35 inches.
Select the dimension of the rectangle that has the same area.

(A) A rectangle with a length of 33 inches and a width of 6 inches.

(B) A rectangle with a length of 30 inches and a width of 25 inches.

(C) A rectangle with a length of 10 inches and a width of 15 inches.

(D) A rectangle with a length of 25 inches and a width of 21 inches.

6.4 Rectangles With The Perimeter and Areas

11 Tim is building a fenced-in area for his cat. The area to be fenced measures 8 feet by 8 feet. How much fencing does he need?

A) 32   B) 30   C) 48   D) 35

12 A rectangle has an area of 88 square feet. If the width of the rectangle is 11 feet, what is the length of the rectangle?

A) 5   B) 7   C) 8   D) 12

13 The perimeter of a rectangle is 70 inches. If the length of the rectangle is 15 inches, what is the area?

A) 15   B) 20   C) 18   D) 12

14 A rectangle has a perimeter of 90 inches. If the width of the rectangle is 16 inches, what is the length of the rectangle?

A) 25   B) 27   C) 29   D) 22

15 The perimeter of a rectangle is 120 inches. If the length of the rectangle is 25 inches, what is the area?

A) 875   B) 850   C) 799   D) 750

16 A rectangle has an area of 250 square feet. If the width of the rectangle is 10 feet, what is the length of the rectangle?

(A) 25   (B) 27   (C) 29   (D) 22

17 The area of a rectangle is 120 square inches. If the length of the rectangle 8 inches, what is the perimeter?

(A) 35   (B) 37   (C) 46   (D) 32

18 The area of a rectangle is 225 square inches. If the length of the rectangle 15 inches, what is the perimeter?

(A) 55   (B) 60   (C) 62   (D) 68

19 The perimeter of a rectangle is 144 inches. If the length of the rectangle is 36 inches, what is the area?

(A) 1260   (B) 1296   (C) 1365   (D) 1268

20 A rectangle has a length of 18 inches and a length of 23 inches. What is the area of the rectangle?

(A) 455   (B) 414   (C) 480   (D) 468

Next Section: Chapter Review ⟫

6.5 Chapter Review

1 A rectangle has 6 rows and 7 columns. How many squares are in the rectangle?

(A) 42 (B) 49 (C) 44 (D) 32

2 What is the area of the rectangle?

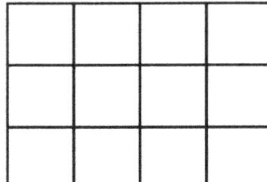

(A) 22 (B) 19

(C) 14 (D) 12

3 What is the missing number in the distributive property equation for the area of the rectangle? $4 \times 4 +$ _____ $= 32$.

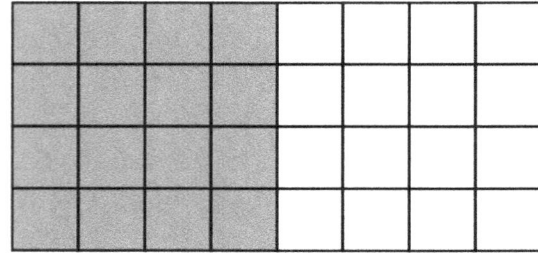

(A) 2 (B) 3

(C) 4 (D) 5

4 A diary measures 15 inches by 20 inches. When the diary is open, it measures 12 inches by 10 inches. What is the area of a computer when the diary is open?

(A) 460 (B) 450 (C) 420 (D) 485

5 The following shape is made of unit squares. Determine the area of the shape.

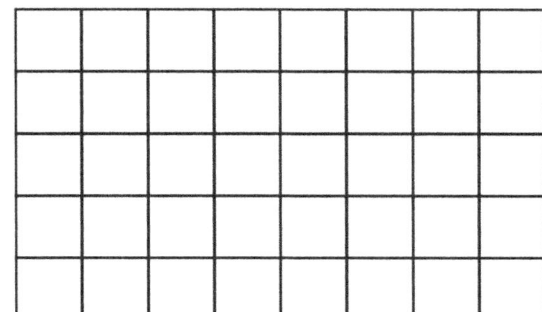

(A) 40   (B) 45

(C) 42   (D) 48

6 What is the perimeter of the figure?

75

27

(A) 206   (B) 204

(C) 200   (D) 290

7 A 5-sided figure has lengths of 35, 78, 68, 92, and 27 feet. What is the perimeter of the figure?

(A) 260   (B) 354   (C) 300   (D) 290

8 What is the perimeter of the figure?

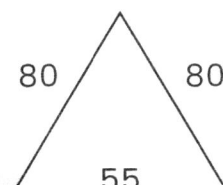

80   80

55

(A) 215   (B) 254

(C) 300   (D) 290

6.5   Chapter Review

9   A curtain is rectangular in shape. If a particular screen is 82 feet wide and 30 feet tall, what is the perimeter of the screen?

   (A) 215   (B) 224   (C) 300   (D) 290

10   What is the perimeter of the figure?

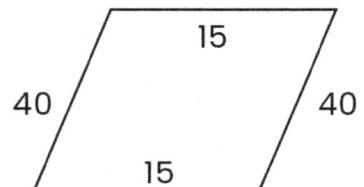

   (A) 115   (B) 124

   (C) 110   (D) 190

11   Robert drew an equilateral triangle (all the sides are the same length). If the length of a side is 120 cm, What is the perimeter of the triangle?

   (A) 485   (B) 360   (C) 500   (D) 525

12   What is the perimeter of an equilateral heptagon with a side length of 25 inches?

   (A) 193   (B) 155   (C) 175   (D) 200

13   A square has a perimeter of 160 inches. What is the length of one side of the square?

   (A) 50   (B) 30   (C) 40   (D) 45

14 A rectangle has a perimeter of 150 mm. The lengths of the 3 sides of the rectangle are 55 mm, 55 mm, and 20 mm. What is the length of the missing side?

(A) 25   (B) 27   (C) 29   (D) 22

15 An equilateral octagon has a perimeter of 440 mm. What is the length of one side of the octagon?

(A) 51   (B) 55   (C) 54   (D) 59

16 An equilateral decagon has a perimeter of 650 inches. What is the length of one side of the decagon?

(A) 65   (B) 64   (C) 67   (D) 60

17 A rectangle has a length of 30 inches and a length of 45 inches. What is the perimeter of the rectangle?

(A) 122   (B) 150   (C) 168   (D) 135

18 A rectangle has an area of 90 square feet. If the width of the rectangle is 10 feet, what is the length of the rectangle?

(A) 10   (B) 7   (C) 8   (D) 9

6.5 Chapter Review

19 The perimeter of a rectangle is 220 inches. If the length of the rectangle is 20 inches, what is the area?

(A) 1500   (B) 200   (C) 1800   (D) 1200

20 A rectangle has a perimeter of 110 inches. If the width of the rectangle is 15 inches, what is the length of the rectangle?

(A) 45   (B) 47   (C) 40   (D) 42

Next Chapter: Shapes ≫

CHAPTER 7

SHAPES

COMPLETE THE PATTERN

UNDERSTANDING ATTRIBUTES OF SHAPES

The attributes of shapes help to identify and classify shapes, compare and contrast them, and understand the properties and relationships between different shapes.

A polygon is a closed figure. This means that each leg of the figure connects to another leg. There are two broad categories of polygons: regular and irregular. A regular polygon is made up of line segments that are all the same length. An irregular polygon can have line segments of different lengths.

Irregular Polygon   Regular Polygon

We commonly refer to different polygons by their number of sides and their properties. A polygon with 3 sides is called a triangle. Based on their sides, there are three types of triangles: equilateral, isosceles, and scalene. An equilateral triangle has 3 equal length sides. An isosceles triangle has two sides of equal length. A scalene triangle has no equal length sides.

Equilateral   Isosceles   Scalene

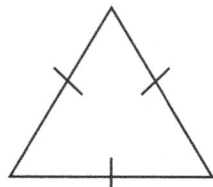
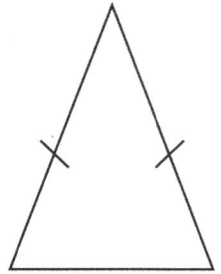
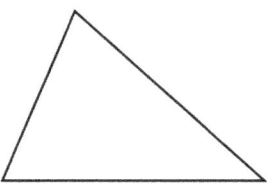

A polygon with four sides is called a quadrilateral. Within the category of quadrilaterals are parallelograms. A parallelogram has two sets of parallel sides. A square is a parallelogram with 4 equal (congruent) sides and 4 right angles. A rectangle is a parallelogram with 2 sets of opposite congruent sides and 4 right angles.

A rhombus is a parallelogram with 4 congruent sides and 2 sets of congruent angles that are opposite each other. A kite is a quadrilateral with two sets of equal-length sides that are adjacent to each other. A trapezoid is a quadrilateral with exactly one set of parallel lines.

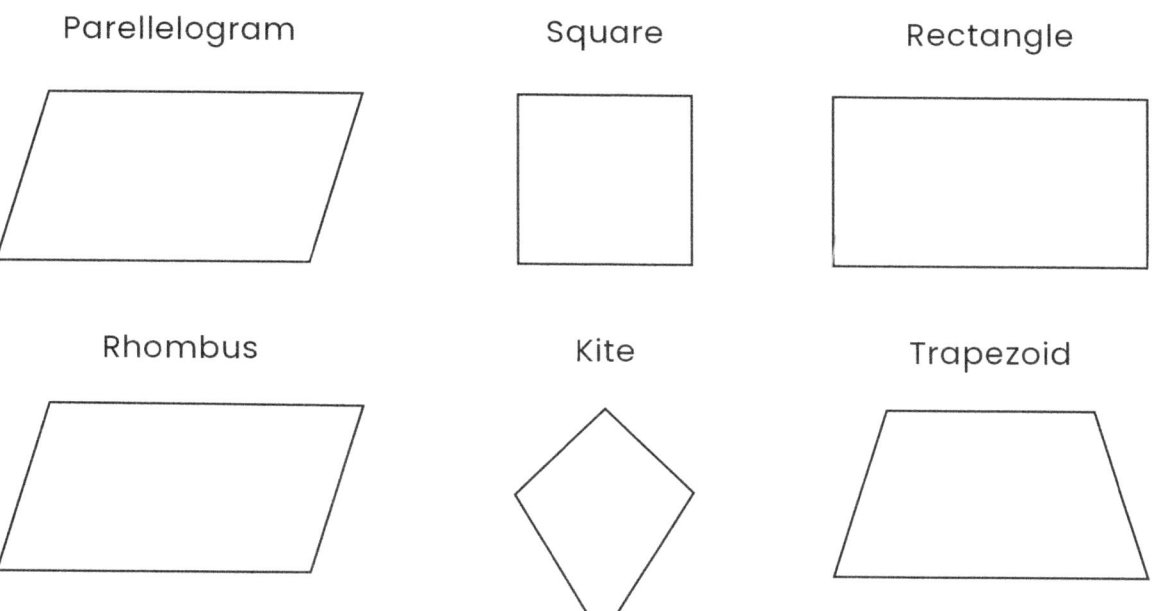

Parellelogram   Square   Rectangle

Rhombus   Kite   Trapezoid

In addition to triangles and quadrilaterals, many shapes are referred to by the number of sides they have. We use the following chart to refer to figures based on their sides.

Number of Slides	Name
5	Pentagon
6	Hexagon
7	Heptagon
8	Octagon
9	Nonagon
10	Decagon

7.1   **Understanding Attributes of Shapes**

1   Which shape is a rhombus?

(A)    (B)    (C)    (D)

2   How many pairs of opposite sides are parallel?

(A) No pairs   (B) 1 pair

(C) 3 pairs   (D) 2 pairs

3   A quilt is constructed of several hexagons. How many sides does each hexagon have?

(A) 7   (B) 6   (C) 8   (D) 9

4   What shape is this?

(A) Hexagon   (B) Rectangle

(C) Square   (D) Pentagon

5 Determine whether the shape is regular or irregular.

(A) Regular   (B) Irregular

6 How many pairs of opposite sides are parallel?

(A) 2 pairs   (B) 1 pair

(C) 3 pairs   (D) No pairs

7 What name best describes this shape?

(A) Right   (B) Isosceles

(C) Scalene   (D) Equilateral

8 A panel of siding has four sides of equal length. What is the siding's shape?

(A) Rectangle   (B) Trapezoid   (C) Kite   (D) Square

7.1   **Understanding Attributes of Shapes**

9   Determine whether the shape is regular or irregular.

(A) Regular   (B) Irregular

10   How many pairs of opposite sides are parallel?

(A) 2 pairs   (B) No pairs

(C) 3 pairs   (D) 1 pair

11   What shape is this?

(A) Triangle   (B) Hexagon

(C) Quadrilateral   (D) Circle

12   How many vertices does this shape have?

_____ vertices.

13 Select the correct name for the polygon.

(A) Kite   (B) Square

(C) Rectangle   (D) Rhombus

14 A street sign has 6 sides. The lengths of the sides are not equal. Is this shape regular or irregular?

(A) Regular   (B) Irregular

15 True or false: Only shapes A and B are parallelograms.

 (A) (B)  (C)

16 Which name does NOT describe this shape?

(A) Square   (B) Quadrilateral

(C) Octagon   (D) Parallelogram

211

7.1   **Understanding Attributes of Shapes**

17   A trapezoid can have a right angle.

(A) True   (B) False

18   A kitchen cabinet door has two sets of opposite sides of equal length and four right angles. What shape is the kitchen cabinet door?

(A) Trapezoid   (B) Square

(C) Rectangle   (D) Rhombus

19   Select the correct name for the figure.

(A) Quadrilateral   (B) Heptagon

(C) Hexagon   (D) Pentagon

20   Jibin cuts a piece of paper into a shape with four sides, with two sets of adjacent equal-length sides. What is the name of the shape he cut?

(A) Square   (B) Pentagon   (C) Hexagon   (D) Kite

Next Section: Quadrilaterals and Non-Quadrilateral

QUADRILATERALS AND NON-QUADRILATERAL

A quadrilateral is a polygon with four sides. A square is a quadrilateral with four equal-length sides and four right angles. A rectangle is a quadrilateral with two sets of equal-length sides opposite each other and four right angles. A trapezoid is a quadrilateral with exactly one pair of parallel lines. A kite is a quadrilateral with two pairs of equal-length sides that are adjacent to each other. A parallelogram is a polygon with two pairs of parallel lines. A rhombus is a parallelogram with equal length sides.

Parellelogram	Square	Rectangle

Rhombus	Kite	Trapezoid

7.2   Quadrilaterals and Non-Quadrilateral

1   To be a kite, a quadrilateral must have sides that are congruent and _____ .

    (A) Adjacent   (B) Opposite   (C) Parallel   (D) Perpendicular

2   What is the name of the figure?

    (A) Square   (B) Rhombus

    (C) Triangle   (D) Kite

3   A trapezoid has exactly one pair of _____ lines.

    (A) Adjacent   (B) Perpendicular   (C) Parallel   (D) Opposite

4   What is the name of the figure?

    (A) Square   (B) Kite

    (C) Rectangle   (D) Quadrilateral

5 The only difference between a rectangle and a square is _____

(A) The length of their sides

(B) The measurement of the interior angles.

(C) The measurement of the exterior angles.

(D) The measurement of opposite angles.

6 A stop sign has 8 equal-length sides. Is a stop sign a quadrilateral?

(A) Yes   (B) No

7 Other than squares, what shape has 4 equal sides?

(A) Kite   (B) Rectangle   (C) Rhombus   (D) Trapezoid

8 What is a quadrilateral?

(A) A closed 2-sided figure   (B) A closed 5-sided figure

(C) A closed 3-sided figure   (D) A Closed 4-sided figure

7.2 Quadrilaterals and Non-Quadrilateral

9 The shape is a quadrilateral.

(A) True

(B) False

10 Susan cuts a rectangle out of a sheet of paper. Since it is a rectangle,

(A) There are two pairs of opposite, congruent sides.

(B) The sides are all same length

(C) The sides are different lengths

(D) Two sides are congruent, and two are not.

11 How many right angles does a rectangle have?

(A) 7　　　　(B) 6　　　　(C) 4　　　　(D) 5

12 Which name does NOT describe this shape?

(A) Quadrilateral　　(B) Polygon

(C) Trapezoid　　(D) Kite

13 Which shape has more sides?

 A    B    C    D

14 Squares and rhombuses have 4 equal length sides.
The difference between the two is the measurement of the interior
_____ .

A) Angles   B) Sides   C) Parallel   D) Perpendicular

15 James says every quadrilateral is a parallelogram.
Do you agree with James? Explain your reasoning.

_____

16 What shape is defined only by two sets of parallel lines?

A) Kite   B) Trapezoid   C) Rhombus   D) Parallelogram

7.2 Quadrilaterals and Non-Quadrilateral

17 The polygon is a quadrilateral.

(A) True   (B) False

18 A rhombus is a parallelogram.

(A) True   (B) False

19 Which shape is a parallelogram?

(A)  (B)   (C)  (D)

20 The door of the cupboard has 4 sides. Is the door a quadrilateral?

(A) Yes   (B) No

Next Section: Partition Shapes Into Parts With Equal Areas

PARTITION SHAPES INTO PARTS WITH EQUAL AREAS

Partitioning means dividing a shape into smaller parts, and in this case, the parts are divided into equal areas.

By partitioning shapes into equal parts, students can visualize how fractions work and how they relate to one another. They can also begin to understand concepts such as equivalent fractions and common denominators.

A fraction is a way to represent parts of a whole. A fraction consists of a numerator and a denominator. The denominator is the total number of equal parts in which the whole is divided. The numerator is the number of those equal parts that we care about.

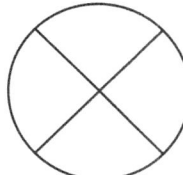 If we shade 3 of the parts of the circle, it looks like the circle below.

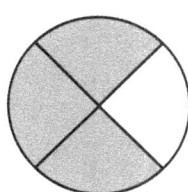 To represent the shaded portion of the circle, we write the fraction $\frac{3}{4}$. The numerator is 3, the number of shaded pieces in the circle. The denominator is 4, the number of equal-sized pieces into which the circle is divided.

Example:

A rectangle is divided into 8 equal parts, and 3 of them are shaded. What fraction of the rectangle is shaded?

We know that there are 8 equal-sized parts, so our denominator is 8.

We are asked about the number of shaded parts, so these are the parts we care about. Therefore, we know the numerator is 3 for the number of shaded parts.

Therefore, the fraction of the rectangle that is shaded is $\frac{3}{8}$.

7.3 Partition Shapes Into Parts With Equal Areas

1 Which shape shows the fraction $\frac{1}{6}$?

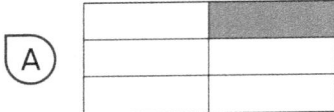

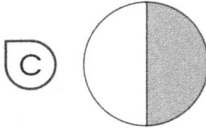
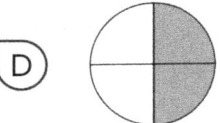

2 What fraction of the shape is not shaded?

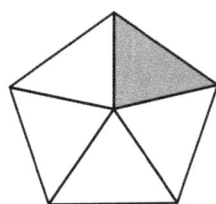

(A) $\frac{2}{3}$ (B) $\frac{4}{3}$

(C) $\frac{4}{5}$ (D) $\frac{3}{5}$

3 A pizza is cut into 8 equal-sized slices. Steffi takes 4 slices of pizza. What fraction of the pizza did she take?

(A) $\frac{1}{8}$ (B) $\frac{4}{8}$ (C) $\frac{2}{8}$ (D) $\frac{3}{8}$

4 Which shape shows the fraction $\frac{2}{5}$?

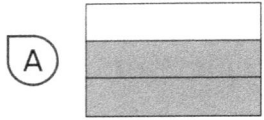

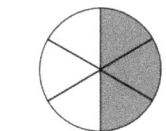

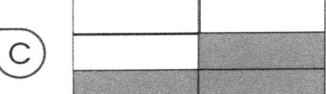

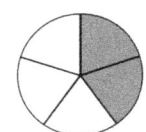

Partition Shapes Into Parts With Equal Areas   **7.3**

5 A hexagon is divided into 6 equal-sized pieces, and 5 of them are shaded. What fraction of the hexagon is shaded?

(A) $\frac{5}{6}$ (B) $\frac{3}{6}$ (C) $\frac{5}{8}$ (D) $\frac{5}{6}$

6 What fraction of the shape is shaded?

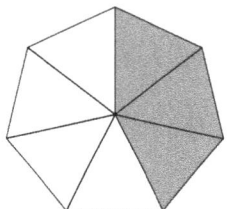

(A) $\frac{1}{7}$ (B) $\frac{4}{7}$

(C) $\frac{3}{7}$ (D) $\frac{3}{5}$

7 Which shape shows the fraction $\frac{2}{4}$?

(A) 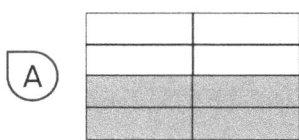   (B)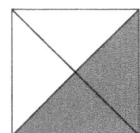

(C) 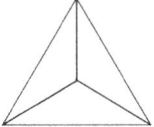   (D)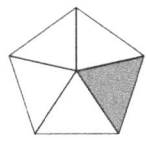

8 An octagon is divided into 8 equal-sized pieces and 5 of them are shaded. What fraction of the octagon is not shaded?

(A) $\frac{1}{7}$ (B) $\frac{4}{7}$ (C) $\frac{3}{7}$ (D) $\frac{3}{8}$

221

7.3 Partition Shapes Into Parts With Equal Areas

9 What fraction of the shape is shaded?

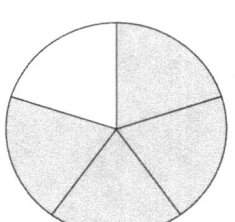

(A) $\frac{4}{5}$ (B) $\frac{1}{5}$

(C) $\frac{3}{7}$ (D) $\frac{3}{5}$

10 **True or False:** The fraction in Model B is greater than the fraction shown in Model A.

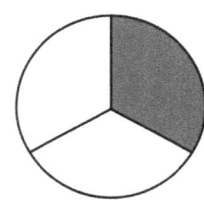 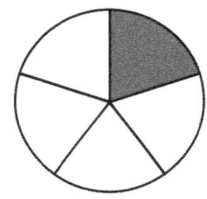

(A) True   (B) False

Model A   Model B

11 There are 10 fruits in a basket, and 4 of them are apples. What fraction of the fruits in the basket are apples?

(A) $\frac{3}{10}$ (B) $\frac{3}{7}$ (C) $\frac{4}{10}$ (D) $\frac{3}{5}$

12 What unit fraction is represented by the shaded area? _____.

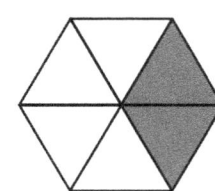

13   Which shape shows the fraction $\frac{2}{5}$?

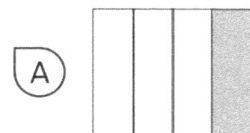

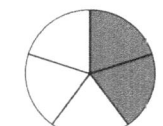

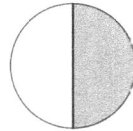

14   What fraction of the shape is shaded?

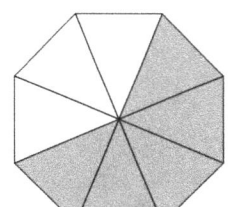

(A) $\frac{4}{5}$ (B) $\frac{1}{8}$

(C) $\frac{3}{8}$ (D) $\frac{5}{8}$

15   A circle is divided into 9 equal-sized pieces, and 5 of them are shaded. What fraction of the circle is not shaded?

(A) $\frac{4}{9}$ (B) $\frac{1}{9}$ (C) $\frac{3}{9}$ (D) $\frac{5}{8}$

16   True or False: The shaded part of this model represents $\frac{5}{8}$.

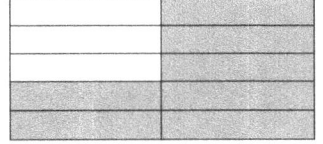

(A) True   (B) False

7.3 Partition Shapes Into Parts With Equal Areas

17 Which shape shows the fraction $\frac{1}{4}$?

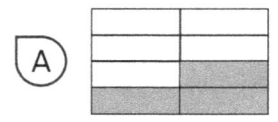 A   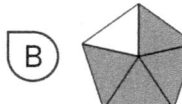 B   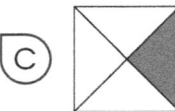 C   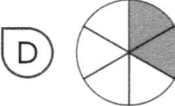 D

18 A bike dealership has 12 of the same bike parked in the sales lot. One week, 7 of the bikes are sold. What fraction of the bikes are sold that week?

A $\frac{4}{12}$ B $\frac{1}{12}$ C $\frac{3}{12}$ D $\frac{7}{12}$

19 What unit fraction is represented by the shaded area?

_____.

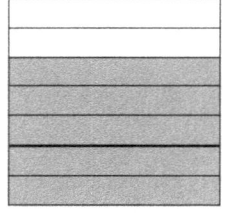

20 What fraction of the shape is not shaded?

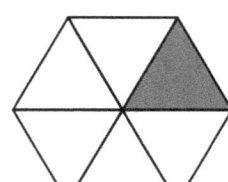

A $\frac{2}{3}$ B $\frac{4}{3}$

C $\frac{4}{5}$ D $\frac{5}{6}$

Next Section: Chapter Review ≫

1 Determine whether the polygon is regular or irregular.

(A) Regular (B) Irregular

2 Which shape is a trapezoid?

 (A)  (B)  (C)  (D)

3 Which quadrilateral has no right angles?

(A) Square (B) Rectangle (C) Rhombus (D) Trapezoid

4 Sherlin is making her own game board. Each piece of the game board has 4 equal-length sides and 4 right angles. What shape are the pieces of the game board?

(A) Kite (B) Rectangle (C) Rhombus (D) Square

7.4   Chapter Review

5   Which name does NOT describe this shape?

- (A) Polygon
- (B) Quadrilateral
- (C) Hexagon
- (D) Parallelogram

6   What fraction of the shape is shaded?

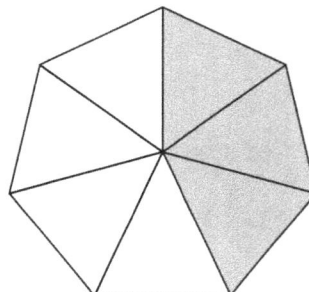

- (A) $\frac{1}{7}$
- (B) $\frac{4}{7}$
- (C) $\frac{3}{7}$
- (D) $\frac{3}{5}$

7   How many vertices does this shape have?

_____ vertices.

8   A specific drill bit has six sides. What is the name of the shape of the bit?

- (A) Hexagon
- (B) Octagon
- (C) Heptagon
- (D) Rectangle

9 Which shape shows the fraction $\frac{1}{5}$?

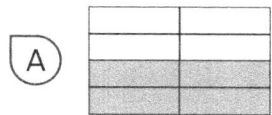 A

 B

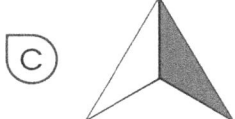 C

 D

10 Francis uses a jigsaw to cut a piece with four sides. What is the name of the piece he cut?

(A) Triangle   (B) Hexagon   (C) Pentagon   (D) Quadrilateral

11 How many pairs of opposite sides are parallel?

(A) No pairs   (B) 1 pair

(C) 2 pairs   (D) 3 pairs

12 In baseball and softball, home plate is the only base with five sides. What shape is the home plate?

(A) Triangle   (B) Square   (C) Hexagon   (D) Pentagon

7.4 Chapter Review

13 What fraction of the shape is not shaded?

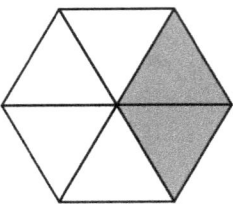

(A) $\frac{4}{6}$ (B) $\frac{1}{5}$ (C) $\frac{3}{7}$ (D) $\frac{3}{5}$

14 A hexagon is cut in half. The resulting shape is a quadrilateral with exactly one set of parallel lines. What shape is the result?

(A) Kite   (B) Rhombus   (C) Trapezoid   (D) Rectangle

15 The polygon is a quadrilateral.

(A) True   (B) False

16 There are 9 equal sized cookies on a platter. Steffi takes the 4 cookies back to her desk. What fraction of cookies did she take to her desk?

(A) $\frac{4}{6}$ (B) $\frac{1}{9}$ (C) $\frac{3}{7}$ (D) $\frac{4}{9}$

17 A parallelogram has _____ sets of parallel lines.

(A) 1   (B) 3   (C) 2   (D) 4

18 True or False: The not shaded part of this model represents $\frac{5}{8}$.

(A) True   (B) False

7.4   **Chapter Review**

19   Which shape has more sides?

(A)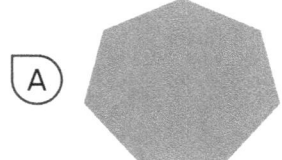

(B)

(C)

(D)

20   What unit fraction is represented by the not shaded area?

(A) $\dfrac{4}{5}$ (B) $\dfrac{1}{8}$ (C) $\dfrac{3}{8}$ (D) $\dfrac{5}{8}$

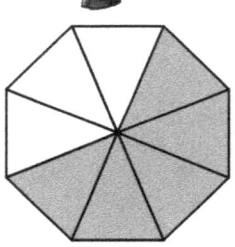

Next Chapter:
Comprehensive Assessment »

COMPREHENSIVE ASSESSMENT

COMPLETE THE PATTERN

1 Lily has 24 shells and puts an equal number of shells into 4 bags. How many shells does Lily put in each bag?

(A) 4   (B) 6   (C) 8   (D) 20

2 Which equation could represent this diagram?

(A) 6 x 6 = 36   (B) 30 ÷ 5 = 6   (C) 6+ 5 = 30   (D) 36 ÷ 6 = 6

3 Mrs. Logan is using 40 pieces of candy to make party favors for Logan's birthday. He puts 5 pieces of candy in each bag. Which equation shows the number of party favor bags Mrs. Logan uses?

(A) 40 ÷ 5 = n   (B) 40 − n = 5   (C) 40 x 5 = n   (D) 5 + n = 40

4 David makes an array using 2 rows of 5 tiles. He adds 3 more rows to the array. Which multiplication sentence does David's array show?

(A) 2 x 10 = 20   (B) 5 x 5= 25   (C) 2 x 4 = 8   (D) 4 x 6 = 24

5 Grace made $ 16 babysitting on Friday and $ 29 babysitting on Saturday. She spent $ 15 for lunch on Sunday. How much money does Grace have left?

(A) $ 31   (B) $ 29

(C) $ 30   (D) $ 28

6 Sarah bakes 4 trays of 11 muffins. She eats 2 for breakfast. Then she gives an equal number of muffins to 6 of her friends. How many muffins does Sarah share with each friend?

(A) 4 (B) 13 (C) 30 (D) 7

7 Luke drew 8 legs on each spider and drew 56 legs. How many spiders did Luke draw? Choose the equation needed to solve this problem.

(A) $56 = n \times 7$ (B) $56 = 8 \times n$ (C) $8 + n = 56$ (D) $56 = 8 \div n$

8 Riley must read a 60-page book. She reads 19 pages on Sunday and then a same number of pages each night for the next 7 days. How many pages does she read each night? Choose the equation to solve this problem

(A) $p = (60 + 19) \div 7$ (B) $p = 60 - 19 - 7$
(C) $(60 - 19) \div 7 = p$ (D) $(60 \div 7) - 19 = p$

9 Max has 4 stacks of 7 books, and Mia has 5 stacks of 6 books. Who has more books? Explain your reasoning.

10 Mr. Jack has 12 books on each shelf. If there are 4 shelves, which expression can be used to determine the number of books Mr. Jack has altogether?

(A) 24 x 2   (B) 24 x 2   (C) 24 x 4   (D) 12 x 12

11 Emily spends 35 minutes each day watching tv. Which expression represents the number of minutes Sarah spends watching tv for 6 days?

(A) 70 x 2   (B) 35 x 35   (C) 70 x 3   (D) 70 x 6

12 June spends 30 minutes on her homework for each subject. On Monday and Tuesday evening, June has homework in mathematics, science, and social studies. How much time does June spend on her homework on Monday and Tuesday?

(A) 120 minutes (B) 180 minutes (C) 40 minutes (D) 100 minutes

13 There are 5 boxes of construction paper in the art room. Three boxes each have 20 sheets of construction paper, and the remaining boxes each have 30 sheets of construction paper. How many sheets of construction paper are in the boxes?

(A) 120 sheets   (B) 150 sheets   (C) 200 sheets   (D) 350 sheets

14 Mr. Mason buys 6 boxes of markers for her students' art projects. 4 of the boxes have 30 markers, and the remaining boxes have 20 markers. How many markers does Mr. Mason buy?

A) 30 markers B) 100 markers C) 140 markers D) 160 markers

15 Cruz reads 24 pages of her book on Monday, 69 pages on Tuesday, and 44 pages on Wednesday. The book has 300 pages. How many more pages does Cruz have to read to finish the book?

A) 163 pages B) 157 pages C) 167 pages D) 367 pages

16 Using the standard algorithm, how would you describe the process of adding these numbers? 208 + 136 = ?

_____

17 Evan and his 5 friends each have $30. Each of them receives an additional 6 from their parents. How much money do they have altogether?

_____

18 Luke exercises for the same amount of time each day. He exercises for 238 minutes six days each week. Approximately how much time does Luke spend exercising each day?

_____

19 Which fraction is modeled on this number line?

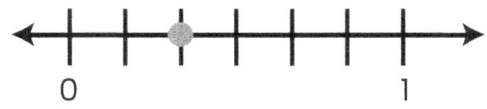

Ⓐ $\frac{1}{6}$ Ⓑ $\frac{1}{3}$ Ⓒ $\frac{2}{5}$ Ⓓ $\frac{1}{5}$

20 The model below represents one whole. What fractional part is shaded?

Ⓐ $\frac{1}{5}$ Ⓑ $\frac{5}{2}$ Ⓒ $\frac{2}{5}$ Ⓓ $\frac{3}{5}$

21 The model below represents one whole. What fractional part is shaded?

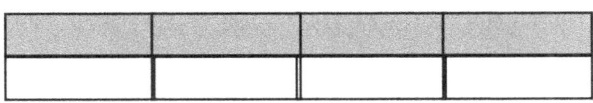

Ⓐ $\frac{8}{4}$ Ⓑ $\frac{8}{2}$ Ⓒ $\frac{2}{8}$ Ⓓ $\frac{4}{8}$

22 Which strategy can be used to generate a fraction that is equivalent to $\frac{7}{9}$.

(A) $\frac{7}{9} + \frac{1}{3}$ (B) $\frac{7}{9} + \frac{2}{3}$ (C) $\frac{7}{9} - \frac{1}{1}$ (D) $\frac{7}{9} \times \frac{3}{3}$

23 What fraction can be used to name the point on this number line?

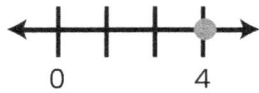

0   4

_____

24 Sarah draws these two fraction models. Each model has the same whole. Which statement describes these models?

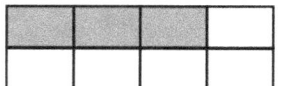 Model A   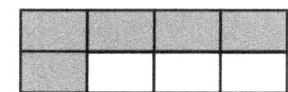 Model B

(A) The shaded part of Model A is less than the shaded part of Model B.

(B) The shaded parts of Model A and Model B are greater than 1.

(C) The shaded parts in Model A and Model B are the same.

(D) The shaded part of Model A is greater than the shaded part of Model B.

25 Mercy draws these two fraction models. Each model has the same whole. Which statement describes these models

 Model A   Model B

(A) The shaded part of Model A is equivalent to the shaded part of Model B.

(B) The shaded part of Model A and Model B are greater than 1.

(C) The shaded part of Model A is less than the shaded part of Model B.

(D) The shaded part of Model A is greater than the shaded part of Model B.

26 Neha colored $\frac{2}{10}$ of this area model. Which fraction is equivalent to $\frac{2}{10}$?

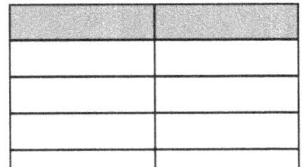   (A) $\frac{1}{10}$ (B) $\frac{2}{5}$ (C) $\frac{1}{5}$ (D) $\frac{5}{2}$

27 The distance between Ava's house and the park is $\frac{2}{5}$ miles. The distance between the park and Ava's school is $\frac{3}{5}$ miles. Which statement correctly describes these distances?

(A) The distance between Ava's house and the park is the greater distance.

(B) The distance between Ava's house and the park is the same as the distance between the park and Ava's school.

(C) The distance between Ava's house and the park is 1 mile more than the distance between the park and Ava's school.

(D) The distance between the park and Ava's school is the greater distance.

28 What is the perimeter of the shape?

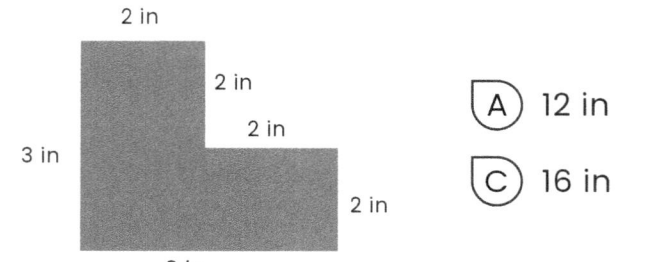

2 in
2 in
2 in
3 in
2 in
3 in

(A) 12 in   (B) 14 in

(C) 16 in   (D) 18 in

---

29 Which is a better unit to describe the volume of a water bottle?

(A) liter   (B) milliliter   (C) kilogram   (D) gram

---

30 True or False: The perimeter of the following shape is 15 ft.

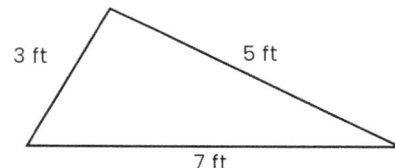

3 ft   5 ft

7 ft

(A) True   (B) False

---

31 True or False: The image of the fish measures 5 inches in length.

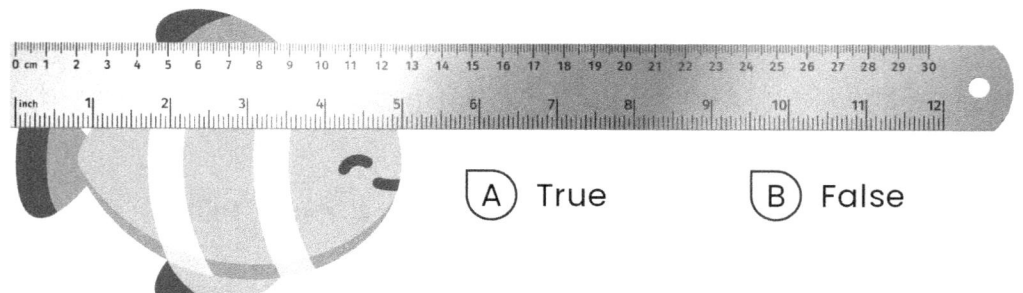

(A) True   (B) False

32 True or False: The area of the shape below is 12 square units. Each square has an area of 1 square unit.

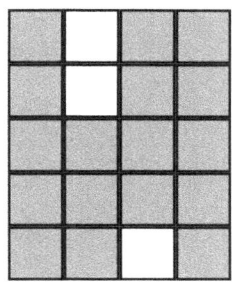

(A) True   (B) False

33 The surface of a rectangular table is 8 feet long and 4 feet wide. What is its area? _____ square feet.

_____

34 What is the length and width of this rectangle?

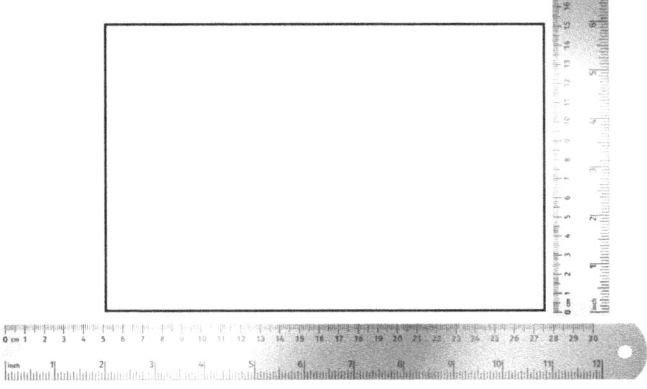

_____

35 Eighty meters is a better estimate for the length of a car key than 80 millimeters.

(A) True   (B) False

36 Which model shows a unit fraction equal to $\frac{1}{5}$?

(A)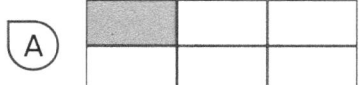

(B)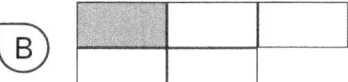

(C)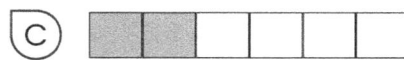

(D)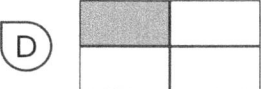

37 James says this model represents $\frac{2}{3}$ because the whole being divided into 3 pieces. Do you agree with James? Explain your reasoning.

 _____

38 Color $\frac{1}{2}$ of each shape

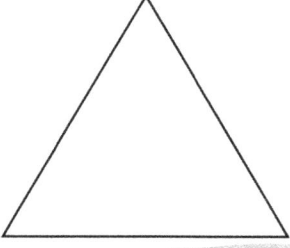

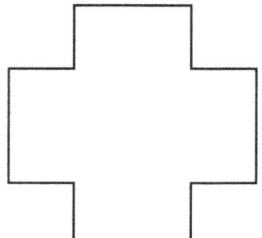

39 What fraction is represented by the model below?

_____

40 Model the unit fraction $\frac{2}{9}$ using the rectangle below.

41 Mercy says these fractions are unit fractions because they all have the same numbers. Do you agree with Mercy?
Explain your reasoning.

$$\frac{1}{4} \qquad \frac{4}{5} \qquad \frac{1}{5}$$

_____

42 Avery draws a model where the unit fraction is $\frac{1}{8}$. How many parts does Avery's model have?

_____

43 How many pairs of parallel sides does this shape have?

44 Lisha cuts this avocado into 3 pieces of equal size. What fraction names the size of one part?

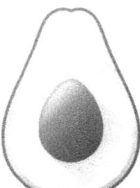

(A) $\frac{2}{3}$ (B) $\frac{1}{2}$

(C) $\frac{3}{2}$ (D) $\frac{1}{3}$

45 Explain why the shaded part of this model represents $\frac{2}{8}$?

_____

Next Chapter: Assessment 2 ≫

COMPREHENSIVE ASSESSMENT

COMPLETE THE PATTERN

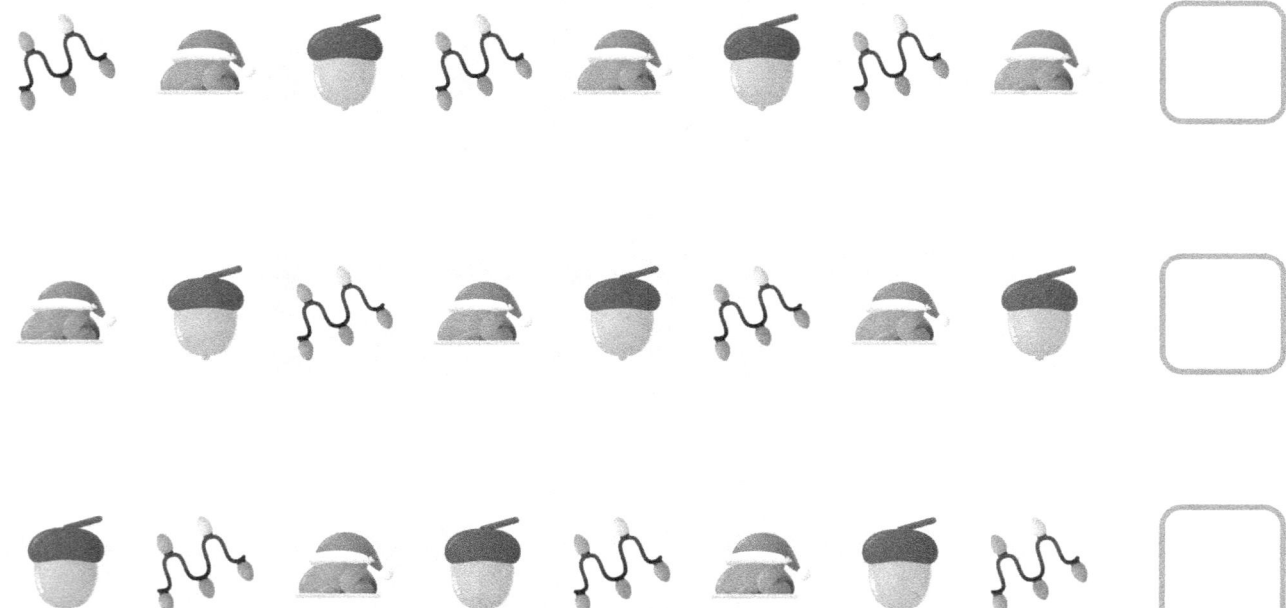

1 Calvin gets 35 new toys. If the toys come in packs of 7, how many packs of toys did Calvin get?

(A) 4   (B) 5   (C) 6   (D) 7

2 Which fraction describes the point on this number line?

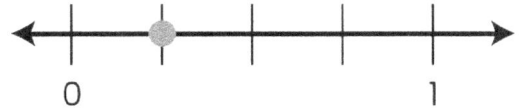

0   1

(A) $\frac{1}{4}$ (B) $\frac{2}{4}$ (C) $\frac{1}{5}$ (D) $\frac{2}{5}$

3 Tanner makes an array using 4 rows of 6 stickers. How many stickers does Tanner have if he adds 2 more rows to the array?

(A) 18   (B) 24   (C) 30   (D) 36

4 Ryker draws a fraction model. Each part has the same area. One part of the model is shaded, and 8 parts are not shaded. What fraction has Ryker modeled?

(A) $\frac{8}{1}$ (B) $\frac{1}{9}$ (C) $\frac{1}{8}$ (D) $\frac{9}{1}$

5 Kate is leaving the school after foot practice. Is it AM or PM?

(A) A.M.   (B) P.M.

247

ASSESSMENT – 2

6 Paul uses a number line to count by 7 to reach 63. If he starts at zero, how many times did Paul count by 7 to reach 63?

(A) 7   (B) 8   (C) 9   (D) 10

7 Complete the equation. $\frac{3}{7}$ = _____.

(A) $\frac{2}{3}$ (B) $\frac{7}{3}$ (C) $\frac{14}{3}$ (D) $\frac{6}{14}$

8 What is the multiplication expression that shows 5 + 5+ 5 + 5 = ?

(A) 3 x 5   (B) 5 x 5   (C) 4 x 5   (D) 5 x 5 x 5

9 Devin shares 8 cookies with each of his 9 friends at lunch. How many cookies did Devin have to share? Choose the equation that represents this problem. Let n represent the total number of cookies.

(A) 8 + 9 = n   (B) n − 9= 8   (C) 8= n ÷ 9   (D) 9 = n x 8

10 Keira has 36 cookies that she places into 9 bags. Which equation can be used to find the unknown factors in this problem?

(A) 36 = 9× 4   (B) 9 x 3 = 27   (C) 9+ 27 = 36   (D) 9 = 36 − 27

11 If there are 60 minutes in 1 hour, how many minutes are in 8 hours and 45 minutes?

(A) 420 min   (B) 745 min   (C) 525 min   (D) 145 min

12 The following shape is made of unit squares. Determine the area of the shape.

(A) 12 square units   (B) 10 square units

(C) 11 square units   (D) 8 square units

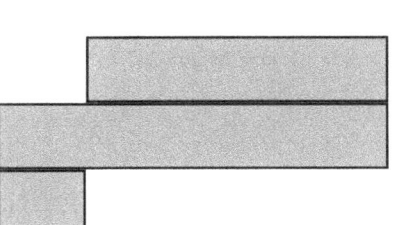

13 Emery's cat has 16 kittens. One-fourth of the kittens have white paws. Which model represents the fraction of kittens with white paws?

 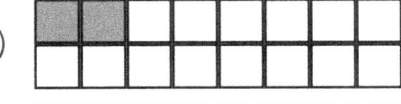   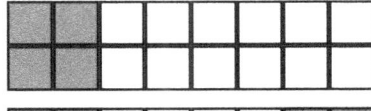

14 Mrs. Derek writes this equation on the board:

$$15 \times 4 = (10 \times 4) + (\underline{\quad\quad} \times 4).$$

What is the missing number that makes this equation true?

(A) 4   (B) 3   (C) 5   (D) 6

15 There are 785 people in Peyton' school. What is this number rounded to the nearest 100?

(A) 800　　　(B) 785　　　(C) 700　　　(D) 750

16 What fraction is equivalent to 7?

(A) $\frac{7}{7}$　　(B) $\frac{1}{7}$　　(C) $\frac{7}{1}$　　(D) $\frac{7}{0}$

17 One day at lunch, a restaurant served 179 burgers, 71 grilled cheese sandwiches, and 58 salads. Which number is the best estimate of the number of meals the restaurant served for lunch that day, rounded to the nearest 10?

(A) 290　　　(B) 300　　　(C) 260　　　(D) 310

18 Gage has 54 slices of pizza left over from a party. He eats 4 slices and divides the rest among 10 containers. Which equation represents the number of slices in each container?

(A) $(54 - 4) \div 10 = s$　　　(B) $(54 - 4) - 10 = s$

(C) $(54 + 4) \div 10 = s$　　　(D) $(54 - 4) \div 4 = s$

19 Dawn covers a figure with square units. Each square has an area of 1 square unit. What is the area of this figure?

(A) 12 square units　　　(B) 13 square units

(C) 14 square units　　　(D) 15 square units

20 Which is a better unit to use for the volume of two raindrops?

(A) liter   (B) milliliter   (C) kilogram   (D) gram

21 What is the area of the rectangle?

6 Units

3 Units

(A) 12 square units   (B) 18 square units

(C) 9 square units   (D) 24 square units

22 Which multiplication equation matches this model?

(A) 4 + 4   (B) 2 x 3

(C) 4 x 4   (D) 4 x 2

23 What is the perimeter of the rectangle?

11 ft

9 ft

(A) 40 ft   (B) 20 ft

(C) 60 ft   (D) 99 ft

24 Daisy is making beaded necklaces. If she uses 20 beads on 4 necklaces, how many beads does she need?

(A) 20 x 4 = 80 beads   (B) 4 + 20 = 24 beads

(C) 20 − 4 = 16 beads   (D) 20 ÷ 4 = 5 beads

25 Jayla needs paper cups for a party. She buys 5 packs of 30 cups. How many paper cups did Jayla buy?

(A) 80 paper cups   (B) 150 paper cups

(C) 120 paper cups   (D) 160 paper cups

26 Where is Point E located?

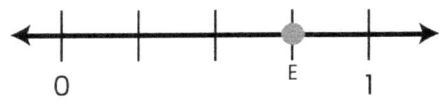

(A) $\frac{1}{3}$ (B) $\frac{3}{1}$ (C) $\frac{3}{4}$ (D) $\frac{4}{3}$

27 In the following recipe for Hot Cocoa, does the recipe call for more sugar or more cocoa?

- 1/3 cup sugar
- 1/4 cup cocoa
- 3 cups milk
- 2 teaspoon vanilla extract

(A) Sugar

(B) Cocoa

28 Nick and Mark are reading the same book.

- The book has a total of 300 pages.
- Nick must read 222 pages to finish the book.
- Mark must read 190 pages to finish the book.

Explain how you would determine the total number of pages Nick and Mark have read.

29 Grace draws this model to show $\frac{2}{6} = \frac{4}{8}$ Do you agree with Sally? Explain your reasoning.

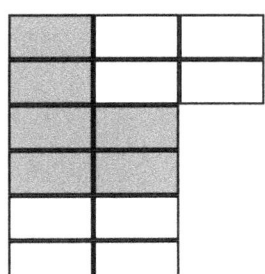

_____

30 Draw a model to show a fraction equivalent to $\frac{3}{9}$.

_____

31 Eden believes this model represents $\frac{2}{3}$
Do you agree with Eden? Explain your reasoning.

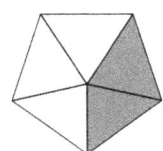 _____

32 Model the division statement 14 ÷ 7.

_____

33 Where is $\frac{1}{4}$ on this number line? Place an "X" on the hashmark that represents $\frac{1}{4}$.

34 Willow's living room is 8 feet wide and 20 feet long. She wants to put a borders around the room. The cost of the border is $2.00 per foot. How much will it cost to buy enough of the border to go around the room?

_____

35 Rebecca did 6 push-ups every day until she reached 42 push-ups. Write a multiplication equation to represent the number of days Rebecca did push-ups.

_____

36 What is the area of the square?

_____ square centimeters

3cm

3cm

37 How can 9 × 9 help you solve 9 × 8?

_____

38 On the number line below, show how many jumps of 8 are needed to reach 48 from 0.

←——————————————————————————————→

Write a multiplication equation that represents this problem.

_____

39 A square mirror has sides that are 7 feet long. What is the mirror's area? _____ square feet

40 What is the length of this sweet corn to the nearest quarter inch?

_____

41 In gym class, the children get into groups of 4 to play a ball game. If there are 10 boys and 30 girls, how many teams are there?

_____

42   Draw two arrays to represent this expression: 5 (2 + 6).

_____

43   The sides of a square-shaped room are 5 yards long. Emily wants to buy carpet to cover the floor of the room. If the carpet costs $10.00 per square yard, how much will it cost to buy enough carpet for the room?

_____

44   How many pairs of opposite sides are parallel?
_____ pairs.

45   Noah believes this model represents $\frac{1}{7}$. Do you agree with Noah? Explain your reasoning.

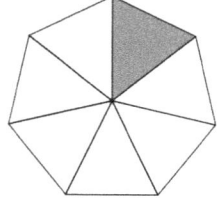

_____

Next Chapter:
Answers and Explanations

ANSWERS AND EXPLANATIONS

TABLE OF CONTENTS

TABLE OF CONTENTS

1. MULTIPLICATION AND DIVISION

1.1 INTERPRET PRODUCTS AND QUOTIENTS OF WHOLE NUMBERS

1. Answer: 9
Explanation:
Addition number sentence: 3 + 3 + 3 = 9
Multiplication number sentence: 3 × 3 = 9.

2. Answer: 3, 4
Explanation:
The picture shows 3 groups of 4 shapes.

3. Answer: D
Explanation: Addition number sentence:
2 + 2 + 2 + 2 + 2 = 10
Multiplication number sentence: 2 × 5 = 10.

4. Answer: Groups into 2 apples ; 2 × 6 = 12
Explanation:

5. Answer: B
Explanation: In the figure, the diamonds are divided into 2 groups. The first group has 4 diamonds, and the second group has only 3 diamonds.

6. Answer: A
Explanation: Note that there are 2 groups and each group contains 5 triangles. There are 10 triangles in all.

7. Answer: B
Explanation: Number of days in a week = 7
Number of weeks = 11
Total number of days = 7 × 11 = 77.

8. Answer: A
Explanation: Count the number of lemons in each group. There are 3 lemons in each group, so you can add 3 + 3 + 3 + 3 to count the total number of lemons.

9. Answer: D
Explanation: Number of days in a month = 30
Number of months = 2
Total number of days = 30 × 2 = 60.

10. Answer: B
Explanation: Each of the brothers gets 5 pancakes, and there are 10 pancakes in total. So, there are 10 ÷ 5 = 2 brothers, and each will need one plate.

11. Answer: D
Explanation: To find the number of cars in each group, you could use the equation 30 ÷ 6 = 5.

12. Answer: C
Explanation: To find the total number of pencils he has; you could use the equation 20 × 5 = 100

13. Answer: A
Explanation: To find the number of cards each player gets, you must do, 48 ÷ 8 = 6 which means each person gets 6 cards.

14. Answer: D
Explanation: To find the number of legs the spiders have together, you must do 4 × 9 = 36 which means the spiders have 36 legs altogether.

15. Answer: B
Explanation: Total number of pastries = 64
Number of people invited = 8
Number of pastries per person = 64 ÷ 8 = 8.

16. Answer: A
Explanation: 6 boxes of 9 pencils are the same as 6 groups of 9 pencils, or counting eight 6 times, so 6 × 9 = 54.

17. Answer: C
Explanation: Total number of apples = 20
Number of baskets = 4, Number of apples in
each basket = 20 ÷ 4 = 5.

18. Answer: 6 books
Explanation: First, to find the total number of
books, you must do 18 + 24 = 42.Then to find
the number of books on each shelf, you must
do 42 ÷ 7= 6.

19. Answer: No, he is incorrect.
Explanation: The model shows 3+3+3+2 that
there are 2 capsicums in the last group. This
model cannot be used for a multiplication
model or repeated addition model because
it does not have equal groups. The model
would have to show 4 groups with 3 peppers
in each group – not 2 peppers in the last
group.

20. Answer: Merlin
Explanation: Merlin bought 3 packs of gum
with 7 pieces in each so think of this as 3
groups of 7, which is 3 × 7 = 21. John bought
4 packs of gum with 5 pieces in each pack,
so think of this as 4 groups of 5 or 4 × 5 = 20.
Using the inequality 21 > 20 to compare the
amounts, Merlin bought more gum.

```
1.2 MULTIPLICATION WITHIN 100
```

1. Answer: B
Explanation: Number of bags = 5
Number of apples in each bag = 12
Total number of apples = 12 × 5
Total number of apples = 60.

2. Answer: A
Explanation: Number of days in a week = 7
Number of weeks = 14
Total number of days in the week = 7 × 14
Total number of days in the week = 98.

3. Answer: D
Explanation: Number of boxes = 23
Number of donuts in each box = 3
Total number of donuts = 23 × 3
Total number of donuts = 69.

4. Answer: B
Explanation: Number of flowers = 4
Cost of each flower = $17
Total cost to be paid = 4 × $17 = $68
Total cost to be paid = $68.

5. Answer: A
Explanation: Number of boxes = 6
Number of pencils in each box = 14
Total number of pencils = 6 × 14
Total number of pencils = 84.

6. Answer: C
Explanation:
Number of cupcakes per person = 4
Number of friends = 16
Total number of cupcakes = 4 × 16
Total number of cupcakes = 64.

7. Answer: B
Explanation: Number of swings = 37
Each swing play = 2
Total number of children playing on the
swings = 37 × 2
Total number of children playing on the
swings = 74.

8. Answer: A
Explanation: Number of rows = 8
Number of brownies in each row = 12
Total number of brownies = 8 × 12
Total number of brownies = 96.

9. Answer: B
Explanation: Number of bags = 11
Cost of each bag = $7
Total Cost spend = 11 × $7
Total Cost spend = $77.

10. Answer: D
Explanation: Number of cars = 13
Number of seats in each car = 4
Total number of people = 13 × 4
Total number of people = 52.

11. Answer: C
Explanation:
Time is taken for one game = 16 minutes
Number of games = 6
Total times taken = 16 × 6
Total time taken = 96 minutes

12. Answer: B
Explanation: Number of tickets to the zoo = 5
Cost per ticket = $16
Total cost of tickets = 5 × $16
Total cost of tickets = $80.

13. Answer: C
Explanation: Number of rows drawn = 7
Strawberries draw in each row = 13
Total strawberries draw = 7 × 13
Total strawberries draw = 91.

14. Answer: A
Explanation: Side of the park= 9meters
Area of the park= side × side = 9 × 9
Area of the park = 81 square meters.

15. Answer: A
Explanation: Number of milkshakes = 2
Number of invited persons = 18 + 6 = 24
Total number of milkshakes = 2 × 24
Total number of milkshakes = 48.

16. Answer: D
Explanation:
Number of matches won by John = 8
Total number of matches won by Daniel = 7 times than John
Total number of matches won by Daniel = 7 × 8
Total number of matches won by Daniel = 56.

17. Answer: B
Explanation: Number of rows = 5
Number of plants in row = 15
Total number of plants = 5 × 15
Total number of plants = 75.

18. Answer: A
Explanation: Cost to save per day = $3
Number of days = 14 days
Total costs saved = $3 × 14
Total costs saved = 42.

19. Answer: D
Explanation: Number of deliveries = 15
Number of weeks = 7 days
Total deliveries = $7 × 15 = 105.

20. Answer: A
Explanation: Number of tables = 9
Number of people per table = 8
Total number of people = 9 × 8
Total number of people = 72.

1.3 DIVISION WITHIN 100

1. Answer: B
Explanation: Number of sandwiches = 50
Each sister gets = 5
Number of sisters = 50 ÷ 5
Number of sisters = 10

2. Answer: A
Explanation: Number of cars = 96
Number of floors = 6
Number of cars on each floor = 96 ÷ 6
Number of cars on each floor = 16.

3. Answer: D
Explanation: Number of friends = 8
Number of donuts for each friend = 48 ÷ 8
Number of donuts for each friend = 6.

4. Answer: B
Explanation: Number of books = 72
Number of shelves = 4
Number of books on each shelf = 72 ÷ 4
Number of books on each shelf = 18.

5. **Answer: A**
Explanation: Number of Ice-creams = 24
Number of Children = 3
Number of Ice-creams for each child = 24 ÷ 3
Number of Ice-creams for each child = 8.

6. **Answer: D**
Explanation: Total length of the rope = 90
Number of friends = 5
Length of rope per friend = 90 ÷ 5
Length of rope per friend = 18.

7. **Answer: C**
Explanation: Number of colored pencils = 78
Number of boxes = 6; Number of colored
pencils in each box = 78 ÷ 6; Number of
colored pencils in each box = 13.

8. **Answer: D**
Explanation: Total number of shirts =
11 + 55 = 66. Total number of shirts = 66
Number of shelves = 6;
Number of shirts on each shelf = 66 ÷ 6;
Number of shirts on each shelf = 11.

9. **Answer: B**
Explanation: Total amount spends = $98
Each balloon cost = $7
Number of balloons purchased = 98 ÷ 7
Number of balloons purchased = 14.

10. **Answer: A**
Explanation: Total number of people = 39 +
30 = 69; Total number of groups = 3
The Number of people in each group = 69 ÷ 3
The Number of people in each group = 23.

11. **Answer: A**
Explanation: Cost has = $100
Each gift cost = $4
Total gift purchase = 100 ÷ 4
Total gift purchase = $25.

12. **Answer: B**
Explanation: Number of classmates = 8
Total time taken = 88 minutes
Time taken for each painting = 88 ÷ 8
Time taken for each painting = 11.

13. **Answer: A**
Explanation: Number of flowers = 36
Number of vase = 6;
Number of flowers in each vase = 36 ÷ 6;
Number of flowers in each vase = 6

14. **Answer: D**
Explanation: Total number of snacks = 35
Candies + 33 cookies
Total number of snacks = 68
Number of brothers = 4
Number of snacks for each brother = 68 ÷ 4
Number of snacks for each brother = 17.

15. **Answer: B**
Explanation: Number of students = 72
Number of teams = 8
Number of students in each team = 72 ÷ 8
Number of students in each team = 9.

16. **Answer: B**
Explanation: Number of cheeseburgers = 69
Number of cheeseburgers that can be
planned to give = 3
Number of people = 69 ÷ 3 = 23
Number of people = 23.

17. **Answer: C**
Explanation: Number of pastries = 84
Number of rows = 7
Number of pastries in each row = 84 ÷ 7
Number of pastries in each row = 12.

18. **Answer: D**
Explanation: Total cost of flowers = $56
Each flower cost = $8
Number of flowers bought = 56 ÷ 8
Number of flowers bought = $7.

19. **Answer: B**
Explanation:
Total area of park = 54 square meters.
Breath of park = 6
Length of the park = 54 ÷ 6
Length of the park = 9.

20. Answer: D
Explanation: Number of pages in a book=100
Number of pages read per day = 10
Number of days to complete the book =
100÷10.
Number of days to complete the book = 10.

```
1.4 MULTIPLICATION AND DIVISION
WITHIN 100 INVOLVING ARRAYS
AND MEASUREMENTS
```

1. Answer: C
Explanation: Number of friends = 12
Number of muffins = 96
Number of muffins per friend = 96 ÷ 12 = 8.

2. Answer: A
Explanation: Length of rope = 48 cm
Number of pieces = 6
Length of each piece = 48 ÷ 6 = 8 cm
Length of 4 such pieces = 8 × 3 = 24cm.

3. Answer: B
Explanation: Number of foxes = 80
Number of dens = 10
Number of foxes in each den = 80 ÷ 10 = 8.

4. Answer: B
Explanation: Total distance = 96 m
Number of rounds = 16
Distance covered in each round =
96 ÷ 16 = 6 m.

5. Answer: D
Explanation: Length of wood for 15 windows =
90 m. ength of wood for each window =
90 ÷ 15 = 6 m. Length of wood for 4 windows
= 6 × 4 = 24 m

6. Answer: B
Explanation: 21 rounds to 20, 19 rounds
to 20, 20 baseball cards + 20 basketball
cards = 40 cards 40 cards 4 = about 10 cards
in each box

7. Answer: A
Explanation: Number of students in a bus = 17
Number of buses = 3
Total number of students = 17 × 3 = 51.

8. Answer: C
Explanation: 48 ÷ 8 = 6,
Larry needs to mow 6 lawns.

9. Answer: B
Explanation: Number of crows = 23
Number of eggs per crow = 3
Total number of eggs = 23 × 3 = 69.

10. Answer: C
Explanation: Total height of the cake = 81 cm
Number of layers = 9
Height of each layer = 81 ÷ 9 = 9 cm

11. Answer: B
Explanation: Add 5 degrees to 72 since the
temperature started at 72 degrees and rose
5 degrees. 72 + 5 = 77 degrees. Then subtract
77 − 67 to find the difference in the afternoon
and night time temperature.

12. Answer: A
Explanation: Number of students = 25
Number of crayons = 100
Number of crayons per student = 100 ÷ 25 =4.

13. Answer: D
Explanation: Length of wood per window
pane = 8 m
Number of window panes = 9
Total length of wood = 8 × 9 = 72 m.

14. Answer: A
Explanation: Aiden works for 4 days, earning
$ 6 a day; multiply to find the amount of
money he made: 4× 6 = $24. The sneakers
cost $ 30, so subtract to determine the
amount of money he needs to buy the shoes:
30 − 24 = $ 6. If he saves $6 a day and needs
6 more dollars, he must save for 1 more day.

15. Answer: B
Explanation: 7 × 5 = 35 and the product in the original problem is 42. To get from 35 to 42 add another group of 7, which is 7 × 6 = 42. 6 × 7 = 42 is the related multiplication fact for 42 ÷ 7 = 6.

16. Answer: D
Explanation: Number of mangoes = 80
Number of trees = 16
Number of mangoes per tree = 80 ÷ 16 = 5.

17. Answer: Yes
Explanation: Yes, a number that is 8 is also divisible by 4 because 8 is a multiple of 4 and 4 is a factor of 8 so if one number can be divided by 8, like 48 8, it can also be divided by 4: 48 ÷ 4.

18. Answer: Answers may vary
Explanation:
24 divided into 4 groups equal 6 in size.

19. Answer: (55−5) ÷ 5 = $10 a day for lunch
Explanation: She started with $55 and has $5 now. Subtract to find the amount of money she spent. 55 − 5 = $50. If she spent 50 over 5 days, divide to find how much money she spent each day. 50 ÷ 5 = 10, she spends $10 each day for lunch.

20. Answer: 26 m
Explanation: Total distance = 78 m
Number of modes = 3. Distance traveled by each mode = 78 ÷ 3 = 26 m.

1.5 CHAPTER REVIEW

1. Answer: 3+3=6; 3×2=6 .
Explanation: Given two groups, each group had three heart shapes.

2. Answer: A
Explanation: To find the total number of milk cans he delivered in a week;
you must do 11 × 5 = 55.

3. Answer: 6 ÷ 2 = 3
Explanation: 3 rows and 2 columns; 3 × 2 = 6.

4. Answer: C
Explanation: Total number of keys = 28
Number of groups = 7
Number of keys in each group = 28 ÷ 7 = 4.

5. Answer: 30 ÷ 6 = 5
Explanation: 6 rows and 5 columns; 6×5 = 30.

6. Answer: B
Explanation: Number of mice = 78
Number of nests = 13
Number of mice in each nest = 78 ÷ 13 = 6.

7. Answer: B
Explanation: There are 5 columns and 4 rows.

8. Answer: D
Explanation: To find how many flowers you put in each vase, you can use the equation 24 ÷ 4 = 6.

9. Answer: A
Explanation: If each tent can sleep 3 people and 15 people are going camping, then 15 ÷ 3 = 5. Use the diagram and circle groups of 3 to represents the 3 people in a tent. 5 groups of 3 people 15 people total. 5 × 3 = 15. so, they need 5 tents for everyone to sleep.

10. Answer: D
Explanation:
Total number of problems = 18 + 24 = 42.
Number of problems in an hour = 7.
Division statement = 42 ÷ ___ = 7
Number of hours = 6.

11. Answer: C
Explanation:
Time is taken to charge a phone = 2 hours.
Total charging hours = 20
Division statement = 20 ÷ ___ = 2
Number of phones = 10.

12. Answer: A
Explanation: Count the number of apples in each group. There are 3 apples in each group, so you can add 3 + 3 + 3 + 3 count the total number of apples.

13. Answer: D
Explanation: Each hour, Logan is paid $ 9 and he works 10 hours, which is the same as counting 10 groups of 9 or 10 × 9 = 90.

14. Answer: B
Explanation: 3 bags with 7 apples in each bag = 3 ×7 = 21 red apples, 4 bags with 6 green apples = 4 ×6 = 24 green apples. So, the total apple is 21 + 24= 45.

15. Answer: D
Explanation: To find the number of friends he has; you must do 30 ÷ 6 = 5.

16. Answer: C
Explanation: First, you must add 36 + 4 + 30 = 70 to find the total number of strings. Then you must divide 70 ÷ 10 = 7. To find the number of friends she will be able to give the bracelets to.

17. Answer: C
Explanation: To solve 63 ÷ 7 = n, think 7 × n = 63 because 63 divided into 7 groups is the same as thinking 7 groups of some number equals 63.

18. Answer: B
Explanation: Think 8 × n = 64 or 64 ÷ 8 = 8 because the cups come 8 in a pack so think how many groups of 8 are needed to get 64 cups? 8 × 8 = 64.

19. Answer: D
Explanation: Number of windows in each house = 12. Total number of windows = 84 Multiplication statement = 12 × ___ = 84 Number of houses = 7.

20. Answer: B
Explanation:
Total number of passengers = 52
Number of taxis = 13
Multiplication statement = 13 × ___ = 52
Number of passengers in each taxi = 4.

2. RELATIONSHIP BETWEEN MULTIPLICATION AND DIVISION

2.1 PROPERTIES OF MULTIPLICATION

1. Answer: B
Explanation: The associative property of multiplication states that when three or more numbers are multiplied, the product is the same regardless of the grouping of the factors. So, 4 × (3 × 8) = (4 × 3) × 8.

2. Answer: (4 x 3) + (4 x 7)
Explanation: The distributive property lets you find a sum by multiplying each addend separately and then adding the products. So, to find a solution for 4×(3+7), We can multiply 4×3 and 4×7 then add them together.

3. Answer: 55
Explanation: 5 x 11 = 55
11 x 5 = 55. Farmer Andrew has 55 plants in each section of his garden.

4. Answer: C
Explanation: The distributive property lets you find a sum by multiplying each addend separately and then add the products.
So, to find a solution for 3 (2 + 3), you can multiplied 3 × 2 and 3 × 3 then add them together.

5. Answer: D
Explanation: The commutative property of multiplication states that you can multiply numbers in any order. So, 4 × 8 is the same as 8 × 4.

6. Answer: A
Explanation: Number of rows = 8
Number of chairs in each row = 7
Number of people = 2
Total number of chairs = $(8×7)×2=56×2=112$.
By the associative property=
$8×(7×2)=8×14= 112$

7. Answer: Array should have 5 rows of 10 or 10 rows of 5
Explanation: The expression is equivalent to $5(10)$ or 50. This can be determined using the distributive property.

8. Answer: C
Explanation: The commutative property of multiplication states that we can multiply numbers in any order. So, $8×5$ is the same as $5 × 8$.

9. Answer: B
Explanation: $12 × (6+a) = 132$
By the distributive property we have,
$(12 × 6) + (12 × a) = 132$;
$12 × a = 132 − 72$; $12a = 60$
$a = 60 / 12$; $a = 5$.

10. Answer: 8
Explanation: $4 × 2 = 8$; $2 × 4 = 8$.

11. Answer: 3 and 5
Explanation: Associative property:
$9 × (3 × 5) = (9 × 3) × 5$.
Missing numbers are 3 and 5.

12. Answer: A
Explanation: Using the distributive property of multiplication $6 × (7 + 2)$ can be written as $(6 × 7) + (6 × 2)$.

13. Answer: C
Explanation: Cost of broccolis = $5
Cost of cabbages = $4, Total cost = $108
By distributive property we have,
$a × (5 + 4) = 108$, $a = 108 / 9$, $a = 12$.

14. Answer: D
Explanation: Number of cupcakes = 18
Number of chocolate chips on each cupcake
= 8. Total number of chocolate chips = $8 × 18$
By the distributive property we have = $8 × (10+8) = (8 × 10) + (8 × 8) = 80 + 64 = 144$.

15. Answer: C
Explanation: By the distributive property:
$7 × c + d = (7 × c) + (7 × d)$.

16. Answer: 12
Explanation: $4 × 3 = 12$;
$3 × 4 = 12$.

17. Answer: D
Explanation: The commutative property of multiplication states that we can multiply numbers in any order.
So, $9 × 5$ is the same as $5 × 9$.

18. Answer: 2 and 7
Explanation: Associative property:
$8 × (2 × 7) = (8 × 2) × 7$.
Missing numbers are 2 and 7.

19. Answer: A
Explanation: Commutative property:
$3 × 9 = 27$, $9 × 3 = 27$, So, it is true.

20. Answer: D
Explanation: Distributive property:
$5 × 4 + 9 = 5 × 13 = 65$,
$5 × 4 + 5 × 9 = 20 + 45 = 65$
$5 × (4+9) = (5 × 4) + (5 × 9)$,
So answer D is correct.

ANSWERS AND EXPLANATIONS

2.2 RELATION BETWEEN MULTIPLICATION AND DIVISION

1. Answer: B
Explanation: Think 9 × n = 72 or 72 ÷ 9 = 8 because the plates come 9 in a pack so think how many groups of 9 are needed to get 72 plates? 9 × 8 = 72.

2. Answer: 60 m
Explanation: Length of the train = 80 m
Number of passenger cars = 8
Length of each passenger car = 80 ÷ 8= 10 m
Length of a train with 6 passenger cars = 6 × 10 m = 60 m

3. Answer: A
Explanation: 15 stickers split into 3 groups means 15 ÷ 3 = 5. The model needs to show 3 groups since the problem is dividing 15 stickers into 3 groups.

4. Answer: C
Explanation: To solve 64 ÷ 8 = n, think 8 × n = 64, because 64 divided into 8 groups, is the same as thinking 8 groups of some number equals 64.

5. Answer: D
Explanation: To determine the total number of beads = 20 + 13 + 27 = 60. Next, divide 60 by 12 to find the number of friends she can give the bracelets to, resulting in 5.

6. Answer: 2 m
Explanation: Length of rope = 120 m
Number of pieces = 15
Length of each piece = 120 ÷ 15 = 8 m
Number of sides on a square = 4
Length of each side = 8 ÷ 4 = 2 m.

7. Answer: A
Explanation: Distance between pool and house = 7 km, Number of travels = 5 × 2 = 10
Total distance traveled = 7 × 10 = 70 km.

8. Answer: 30 m
Explanation: Total distance = 120 m
Number of people = 4, Distance covered by each person = 120 ÷ 4 = 30 m

9. Answer: A
Explanation: Weight of each apple = 180 g
Number of apples = 5. Total weights of 5 apples = 5 × 180 = 900 g.

10. Answer: 26L
Explanation: Number of jugs = 13
Capacity of each jug = 2L
Total capacity = 13 × 2 = 26L

11. Answer: B
Explanation: Total height of the cake = 96 cm
Number of layers = 6
Height of each layer = 96 ÷ 6 = 16 cm

12. Answer: 2 cm
Explanation: Length of rope = 84 cm
Number of hexagons = 84 ÷ 7 = 12 cm
Number of sides on a hexagon = 6
Length of each side = 12 ÷ 6 = 2 cm

13. Answer: B
Explanation: Length of 6 drawing books = 54 cm, Length of each book = 54 ÷ 6 = 9 cm
Length of 11 drawing books = 9 × 11 = 99 cm

14. Answer: C
Explanation: The first expression (5 × 7) represents the total number of color boxes Jessy starts with; she then gives away 10 boxes (−10) and receives 5 more boxes (+ 5).

15. Answer: A
Explanation: 7×5 is the same as (7×3)+(7×2) because 5 can be split into two addends 3+2, multiply each by 7 and then add the products together to get the final product.

16. Answer: B
Explanation: $72 is the total amount of money spent, each orange costs $8, so divide to find the number of oranges 72 ÷ 8 = 9.

17. Answer: C
Explanation: Steffi can multiply 7×8 which is one more group of 7 than 7×7. Then subtract one group of 7 to get the same answer as 7×7. 7 × 8 and subtract one group of 7, 7 × 8 = 56 − 7 = 49, 7 × 7 = 49.

18. Answer: D
Explanation: Total cost of balloons = $70
Cost of each balloon = $2
Number of balloons = 70 ÷ 2 = 35

19. Answer: A
Explanation: Total number of times the bell rang = 52. Number of rings per customer = 2
Number of happy customers = 52 ÷ 2 = 26

20. Answer: 48 cm
Explanation: Height of 15 bricks = 90 cm
Height of each brick = 90 ÷ 15 = 6 cm
Height of 8 bricks = 6 × 8 = 48 cm

2.3 CHAPTER REVIEW

1. Answer: A
Explanation: Cost of jersey = $10
Cost of short = $7, Number of sets = 6,
By distributive property,
we have = 6 × (10+7) = 6 × 17 = 102.

2. Answer: B
Explanation: Weight of each orange = 120 g
Number of oranges = 7. Total weights of 7 oranges = 7 × 120 = 840 g.

3. Answer: 6 and 8
Explanation: Associative property:
7 × (6 × 8) = (7 × 6) × 8.
Missing numbers are 6 and 8.

4. Answer: D
Explanation: 20 stickers split into 4 groups means 20 ÷ 4 = 5. The model needs to show 4 groups since the problem is dividing 20 stickers into 4 groups.

5. Answer: C
Explanation: Number of baskets = 9
Number of fruits on each basket = 5
Total number of fruits = 9 × 5 = 45
By commutative property = 5 × 9 = 45

6. Answer: D
Explanation: Associative Property of multiplication states that when three or more numbers are multiplied, the product is the same regardless of the grouping of the factors. So, 4 × (7 × 13) = (4 × 7) × 13

7. Answer: B
Explanation: Consider the number 7. If we let n = 63 or 63 ÷ 7 = 9, we can see that it takes 9 groups of 7 cups each to obtain a total of 63 cups.

8. Answer: (7 × 2) + (7 × 6)
Explanation: The distributive property allows for finding a sum by multiplying each term separately and then adding the products. In the case of 7 × (2 + 6), you can multiply 7 × 2 and 7 × 6 individually, and then add the two products together to obtain the solution.

9. Answer: A
Explanation: Distance between the tennis court and house = 5 km,
Number of travels = 6 × 2 = 12,
Total distance traveled = 5 × 12 = 60 km

10. Answer: C
Explanation: Since one pack has 6 bike toys, you would need to divide 42 by 6 to find the number of packs. 42 ÷ 6 = 7 packs.

11. Answer: 6
Explanation: Commutative property:
3 × 2 = 6; 2 × 3 = 6.

12. Answer: B
Explanation: Length of rope = 100 cm
Number of pentagons = 100 ÷ 5 = 20 cm
Number of sides on a pentagon = 5
Length of each side = 20 ÷ 5 = 4 cm.

269

ANSWERS AND EXPLANATIONS

13. Answer: A
Explanation: Number of boxes = 7
Number of chocolates in each box = 6
Number of people = 2, Total number of
chocolates = $(7×6)×2 = 42×2 = 84$; By the
associative property = $7×(6×2) = 7×12 = 84$.

14. Answer: D
Explanation: 4 rows + 3 rows = 7 rows;
7 rows × 7 equals 49.

15. Answer: C
Explanation: The distributive property lets
you find a sum by multiplying each addend
separately and then adding the products. So,
to find a solution for $2(3+4)$, you can multiply
2×3 and 2×4 then add them together.

16. Answer: A
Explanation: Counting by seven to 63 is the
same as counting groups of 7 to 63;
$7×n = 63$ or $63÷7 = n$. $7×9 = 63$, so Angelina
counted by seven 9 times to get to 63 on the
number line.

17. Answer: D
Explanation: The commutative property
of multiplication states that the order of
numbers being multiplied can be changed
without affecting the result.
Therefore, 7 × 6 is equivalent to 6 × 7.

18. Answer: 48 cm
Explanation: Height of 12 blocks = 96 cm
Height of each block = 96 ÷ 12 = 8 cm
Height of 6 bricks = 8 × 6 = 48 cm.

19. Answer: C
Explanation: Cost of strawberries = $4
Cost of kiwis = $6, Total cost = $90 By
distributive property we have,
$a × (4 + 6) = 90$; $a = 90/10$; $a = 10$.

20. Answer: 40 m
Explanation: Length of wood for 12 windows =
60 m, Length of wood for each window =
60÷12 = 5m, Length of wood for 8 windows =
5×8=40 m.

270

3. PLACE VALUE

3.1 ROUND WHOLE NUMBERS TO THE NEAREST 10 OR 100

1. Answer: C
Explanation: The hundredth place is three
places to the left of the decimal.

2. Answer: B
Explanation: 700 + 50 +3.

3. Answer: A
Explanation:
$7 ≥ 5$ so we round 6 to 7 and fill in with 0s.

4. Answer: D
Explanation:
$3 < 5$ so we keep 1 and fill in with 0s.

5. Answer: B
Explanation: 900 - 300 = 600.

6. Answer: A
Explanation: 600 + 600 = 1,200.

7. Answer: C
Explanation: 155 can be rounded to 160

8. Answer: D
Explanation: 309 rounded to the nearest
hundred is 300.

9. Answer: B
Explanation: Ari harvests between 700 and
800 carrots, so the number must be less than
800 or close to it.

10. Answer: C
Explanation: The number of oranges is
between 500 and 600 but rounded to the
nearest ten must be 500.

11. Answer: A
Explanation: $62 ≈ 60$ and $19 ≈ 20$ so 60 + 20 =
80. So, Brenden has about 80 stamps.

12. Answer: D
Explanation: 23 is closer to 0 than 100.

13. Answer: B
Explanation: 175 can be rounded to 180.

14. Answer: A
Explanation: 298 rounded to the nearest ten is 300.

15. Answer: C
Explanation: 2,101 can be rounded to the nearest 2,000.

16. Answer: D
Explanation: The number 1,915 rounded to the nearest hundred is 1900.

17. Answer: 440 teddy bears
Explanation: 444 can be rounded to 440.

18. Answer: 5,000 birds stickers
Explanation: 4,969 rounded to the nearest hundred is 5,000

19. Answer: Answer may vary
Explanation: Levi could have been between 45 and 55 notebooks. If Kyle has 14 fewer notebooks, he could have more 31 and 45 stickers.

20. Answer: 430 bikes.
Explanation: 432 can be rounded to 430

3.2 ADD AND SUBTRACT WITHIN 1000

1. Answer: B
Explanation: Student demonstrates an understanding of the equal sign as a symbol showing both expressions should have the same value. 521 + 326 − 287 = 560.
560 − 208 = 352.

2. Answer: D
Explanation: Student uses the associative property to show the number of Ice creams eaten by both friends and subtracts the number of ice creams eaten by Miller. The equation will be 150 − 40 − 40 − 20 which is same as 150 − (40+40) − 20.

3. Answer: 138
Explanation: The student may use strategies based on place value and the properties of operations to group numbers in different ways. 909 − 790 + 206 − 187 = 138.

4. Answer: A
Explanation:
878 - 357 = 800 + 70 + 8 - 300 + 50 + 7 = 521

5. Answer: C
Explanation:
295 - 182 = 200 + 90 + 5 - 100 + 80 + 2 = 113

6. Answer: D
Explanation:
354 - 111 = 300 + 50 + 4 - 100 + 10 + 1 = 243

7. Answer: 494
Explanation:
216 + 278 = 200 + 10 + 6 + 200 + 70 + 8 = 494

8. Answer: B
Explanation:
399 + 428 = 300 + 90 + 9 + 400 + 20 + 8 = 827

9. Answer: 424 watermelons
Explanation:
875 - 451 = 800 + 70 + 5 - 400 + 50 + 1 = 424

10. Answer: 231
Explanation:
381 - 150 = 300 + 80 + 1 - 100 + 50 + 0 = 231

11. Answer: C
Explanation:
178 + 215 = 100 + 70 + 8 + 200 + 10 + 5 = 393

12. Answer: A
Explanation:
289 + 587 = 200 + 80 + 9 + 500 + 80 + 7 = 876

13. Answer: 599
Explanation:
897 − 298 = 800 + 90 + 7 − 200 + 90 + 8 = 599

14. Answer: D
Explanation:
558 − 252 = 500 + 50 + 8 − 200 + 50 + 2 = 306

15. Answer: A
Explanation:
256 + 256 = 200 + 50 + 6 + 200 + 50 + 6 = 512

16. Answer: B
Explanation:
466 − 214 = 400 + 60 + 6 − 200 + 10 + 4 = 252

17. Answer: 426
Explanation:
778 − 352 = 700 + 70 + 8 − 300 + 50 + 2 = 426

18. Answer: C
Explanation: 984 − 625 = 359

19. Answer: 372
Explanation:
175 + 197 = 100 + 70 + 5 + 100 + 90 + 7 = 372

20. Answer: D
Explanation:
824 − 568 = 800 + 20 + 4 − 500 + 60 + 8 = 256

3.3 MULTIPLY ONE – DIGIT WHOLE NUMBERS BY MULTIPLES OF 10

1. Answer: A
Explanation:
5 tens are the same as 5 groups of 10.
5 groups of 10 or 5 × 10 = 50.
Repeated addition 10 + 10 + 10 + 10 + 10 = 50.

2. Answer: C
Explanation: Six $ 10 tickets are the same as 6 groups of 10 or 6 × 10 = 60.
Count repeated groups:
10 + 10 + 10 + 10 + 10 + 10 = 60.

3. Answer: B
Explanation: 4 × 10 is the same as 4 group of 10 or 4 boxes with 10 candies on each box.

4. Answer: 180
Explanation: 3 school buses with 60 students in each bus = 3 × 60 = 180. or count repeated groups 60 + 60 + 60 = 180.

5. Answer: 10 × 7 = 70
Explanation: If Calvin shares the 70 pencils with 7 friends, they will each get 10 pencils because 10 × 7 = 70.

6. Answer: A
Explanation:
8 tens are equal to 80 because 8 × 10 = 80.
9 tens are equal to 90 because 9 × 10 = 90.
2 tens are equal to 20 because 2 × 10 = 20.
$80 + $90 + $20 = $190.

7. Answer: D
Explanation: 11 packs of 40 cups is the same as 11 × 40 = 440
11 × 4 = 44 so 11 × 40 = 440.

8. Answer: $130
Explanation: Thirteen 10s is the same as 13 groups of 10 or 13 × 10. Since Elliot has thirteen $10 bills, 13 × $10 = $130.

9. Answer: B
Explanation: 7 packs of 80 strawberries is the same as counting 80 × 7 times or multiplying 80 × 7 = 560. Another way to solve is to break it apart 80 into 10 × 8 then multiply by 7: 7 × 8 × 10 = 560.

10. Answer: C
Explanation: If each hour is 60 minutes, then is 12 hours × 60 minutes in 1 hour = 720 minutes. Then add 10 minutes to 720 minutes. 720 + 10 = 730 minutes

11. Answer: B
Explanation: 5 tens = 50.

12. Answer: 90
Explanation: 9×10 = 9×1 tens = 9 = tens = 90.

13. Answer: C
Explanation: 5×30 = 5×3 tens= 15 = tens = 150

14. Answer: A
Explanation:
3×40 = 3×4 tens = 12 = tens = 120.

15. Answer: B
Explanation: If each hour is 60 minutes, then is 5 hours × 60 minutes = 300

16. Answer: D
Explanation: 6×70=6×7 tens=42 = tens=420.

17. Answer: C
Explanation: 5×50=5×5 tens=25 = tens=250.

18. Answer: 160
Explanation: 4×40=4×4 tens=16 = tens=160.

19. Answer: 240
Explanation: 3×80=3×8 tens=24 = tens=240.

20. Answer: B
Explanation: 4×20=4×2 tens=8 = tens=80.

3.4 CHAPTER REVIEW
---

1. Answer: D
Explanation: 188 red cars can be rounded to 200 and 312 blue cars can be rounded to 300. So, the estimated total number of cars is 200 + 300 = 500.

2. Answer: A
Explanation: Enzo has about 70 watches as 73 rounds to 70. His brother gives him about 30 more watches as 27 rounds to 30. He knows about 70 + 30 = 100 watches.

3. Answer: $900
Explanation: $378 can be rounded to $400 and $514 can be rounded to $500. The total amount of money rounded to the nearest hundred is $900.

4. Answer: B
Explanation: Rounded to the nearest hundred, one person has 2,500 sheep and another person has 4,700 sheep. So, together they have 2,500 + 4,700 = 7,200 sheep.

5. Answer: A
Explanation: 63 can be rounded to 60 and 36 can be rounded to 40. The total rounded to the nearest ten is 60 + 40 = 100.

6. Answer: 900
Explanation: 496 can be rounded to 500 and 438 can be rounded to 400. The total number of students, rounded to the nearest hundred is 500 + 400 = 900.

7. Answer: D
Explanation: Rounding each value to the nearest hundred: 800 and 300.
The total is 800 + 300 = 1100.

8. Answer: B
Explanation: Rounding each value to the nearest ten: 300 and 170.
300 + 170 = 470.

9. Answer: 180 gifts
Explanation: Rounded to the nearest ten, she received approximately 180 gifts.

10. Answer: C
Explanation: Add $175 he received from his father to his money $369. Then subtract the amount of $216 he spends it on a new bicycle. 369 + 175 - 216 = 328.

11. Answer: A
Explanation: The one's place is one place to the left of the decimal.

12. Answer: C
Explanation: 100 + 7.

13. Answer: 2,300
Explanation: 2,267 rounded to the nearest hundred is 2,300

14. Answer: D
Explanation: The number 3,278 rounded to the nearest hundred is 3,300.

15. Answer: B
Explanation: Student demonstrates an understanding of the equal sign as a symbol showing both expressions should have the same value. 391 + 276 − 257 = 410.
410 − 178 = 232.

16. Answer: 271 cats
Explanation:
682 - 411 = 600 + 80 + 2 - 400 + 10 + 1 = 271.

17. Answer: A
Explanation: 1 tens are the same as 1 group of 10.
1 group of 10 or 1 × 10 = 10.

18. Answer: D
Explanation: 6 × 10 is the same as 6 groups of 10 or 6 boxes with 10 spoons on each box.

19. Answer: C
Explanation: 4 packs of 70 are tomatoes is the same as counting 70, 4 times or multiplying 70 × 4 = 280. Another way to solve is to break apart 70 into 10 × 7 then multiply by 4:
4 × 7 × 10 = 280.

20. Answer: B
Explanation: 1 tens = 10.

4. FRACTIONS

4.1 DIVIDING "A" WHOLE INTO "B" PARTS AND A/B FRACTIONS

1.Answer: D
Explanation: The denominator is the bottom number of the fraction's and the number of parts into which the whole was split.

2. Answer: B
Explanation: The numerator is the top number of the fraction's and the number of pieces of the whole we have.

3. Answer: C
Explanation: There are 8 squares, and 4 are shaded.

4. Answer: B
Explanation: There are 10 squares, and 6 are shaded.

5. Answer: A
Explanation: There are 4 squares, and 1 is shaded.

6. Answer: A
Explanation: $\frac{4 \div 2}{8 \div 2} = \frac{1}{2}$

7. Answer: A
Explanation: $\frac{1 \times 6}{4 \times 6} = \frac{6}{24}$

8. Answer: D
Explanation: $\frac{5\times2}{4\times2} = \frac{10}{8}$
If we decrease the number of parts we have to 5, we must also decrease the number of parts of the whole to 4.

9. Answer: C
Explanation: *We divide the number of slices eaten (the number of parts we have) by the total number of slices (parts of the whole).*

10. Answer: A
Explanation: *We write the number of red balls (number of parts we have) over the total number of balls (parts of the whole).*

11. Answer: B
Explanation: *We write the number of burned-out bulbs (number of parts we have) over the total number of lights (parts of the whole).*

12. Answer: D
Explanation: *We write the number of gold (number of parts we have) over the total number of fish (parts of the whole).*

13. Answer: B
Explanation: *We divide the number of kids wearing black shoes (parts we have) by the total number of kids in the group (parts of the whole).*

14. Answer: A
Explanation: *We divide the number of animals bought that are dogs (number of parts we have) by the total number of animals bought (parts of the whole).*

15. Answer: B
Explanation: *We write the number of pink bedrooms (number of parts we have) over the total number of bedrooms (parts of the whole).*

16. Answer: B
Explanation: $\frac{2\times7}{3\times7} = \frac{14}{21}$

17. Answer: B
Explanation: *If we decrease the number of parts of the whole that exist to 5, we must also decrease the parts of the whole that we have to 4.*

18. Answer: C
Explanation: There are 12 squares and 11 are shaded.

19. Answer: C
Explanation: *We write the number of white tigers (parts we have) over the number of tigers at the zoo (parts of the whole).*

20. Answer: D
Explanation: *If we increase the number of the parts of the whole to 14, we must also increase the number of parts that we have to 2.*

4.2 FRACTIONS ON THE NUMBER LINE

1. Answer: B
Explanation: *We write the number of books checked out (the number of parts we have) over the total number of books (the total number of parts)*

2. Answer: D
Explanation: *We write the number of torn bags (the number of parts we have) over the total number of new bags (the total number of parts).*

3. Answer: D
Explanation: *We write the number of baby bones in (the number of parts we have) over the total number of bones (the total number of parts).*

4. Answer: B
Explanation: *We write the number of doughnuts eaten (number of parts we have) over the number of doughnuts available (the total number of parts).*

5. Answer: B
Explanation: *We write the number of occupied rings (the number of parts we have) over the total number of rings (the total number of parts).*

6. Answer: A
Explanation: *We write the number of rotten apples (the number of parts we have) over the total number of apples (total number of parts).*

7. Answer: A
Explanation: *We write the number of ice creams ate (the number of parts we have) over the total number of ice creams (total number of parts).*

8. Answer: A
Explanation: *There are 3 lines that equally divide the number into 4 pieces.*

9. Answer: B
Explanation: *The dot is shown in 6th line that equally divide the number into 8 pieces.*

10. Answer: B
Explanation: *The dot is shown in 2nd line that equally divide the number into 5 pieces.*

11. Answer: D
Explanation: *The dot is shown in 1st line that equally divide the number into 4 pieces.*

12. Answer: C
Explanation: *The dot is shown in 8th line that equally divide the number into 10 pieces.*

13. Answer: C
Explanation: *The dot is shown in 1st line that equally divide the number into 10 pieces.*

14. Answer: A
Explanation: *We divide the number of animals bought that are dogs (number of parts we have) by the total number of animals bought (parts of the whole).*

15. Answer: C
Explanation: *The dot is shown in 10th line that equally divide the number into 20 pieces.*

16. Answer: B
Explanation: *We write the number of kids with blue caps (the number of parts we have) over the total number of kids (total number of parts).*

17. Answer: B
Explanation: *We write the number of thriller movies (the number of parts we have) over the total number of movies (total number of parts).*

18. Answer: A
Explanation: *We write the number of sandwiches sold (the number of parts we have) over the total number of sandwiches (total number of parts).*

19. Answer: A
Explanation: *We write the number of comic novels (the number of parts we have) over the total number of novels (total number of parts).*

20. Answer: A
Explanation: *If we increase the number of parts of the whole to 14, we must also increase the number of parts that we have to 2.*

4.3 EQUIVALENT FRACTIONS

1. Answer: C
Explanation: Remaining all options are equivalent to $\frac{1}{4}$ Only $\frac{1}{4} \neq \frac{2}{4}$

2. Answer: C
Explanation: Remaining all options are equivalent to $\frac{2}{5}$ Only $\frac{2}{5} \neq \frac{4}{5}$

3. Answer: A
Explanation: $\frac{1 \times 3}{3 \times 3} = \frac{3}{9}$

4. Answer: D
Explanation: $\frac{3 \times 5}{5 \times 5} = \frac{15}{25}$

5. Answer: B
Explanation: $\frac{4 \div 2}{10 \div 5} = \frac{2}{5}$

6. Answer: A
Explanation: $\frac{4\times3}{5\times3} = \frac{12}{15}$

7. Answer: A
Explanation: $\frac{5\times2}{7\times2} = \frac{10}{14}$

8. Answer: B
Explanation: $\frac{2}{3} \neq \frac{4}{7}$

9. Answer: B
Explanation: $\frac{3}{12} = \frac{x}{6}$, $\frac{3\div3}{12\div3} = \frac{1}{6}$

10. Answer: A
Explanation: $\frac{5}{15} = \frac{x}{30}$, $\frac{5\times2}{15\times2} = \frac{10}{30}$

11. Answer: A
Explanation: $\frac{4}{9} = \frac{8}{x}$, $\frac{4\times2}{9\times2} = \frac{8}{18}$

12. Answer: B
Explanation: $\frac{3}{27} = \frac{1}{x}$, $\frac{3\div3}{27\div3} = \frac{1}{9}$

13. Answer: B
Explanation: $\frac{4}{14} = \frac{2}{x}$, $\frac{4\div2}{14\div2} = \frac{2}{7}$

14. Answer: A
Explanation: $\frac{5}{13} = \frac{x}{26}$, $\frac{5\times2}{13\times2} = \frac{10}{26}$

15. Answer: C
Explanation: $\frac{18}{48} = \frac{x}{8}$, $\frac{18\div6}{48\div6} = \frac{3}{8}$

16. Answer: A
Explanation: $\frac{5\times7}{9\times7} = \frac{35}{63}$

17. Answer: B
Explanation: $\frac{8\div2}{14\div2} = \frac{4}{7}$

18. Answer: B
Explanation: $\frac{2}{7} \neq \frac{4}{11}$

19. Answer: B
Explanation: $\frac{80}{30} = \frac{x}{6}$, $\frac{80\div5}{30\div5} = \frac{16}{6}$

20. Answer: C
Explanation: $\frac{6}{18} = \frac{1}{x}$, $\frac{6\div6}{18\div6} = \frac{1}{3}$

4.4 EXPRESS WHOLE NUMBERS AS FRACTIONS

1. Answer: A
Explanation: We can write any whole number as a fraction over 1.

2. Answer: B
Explanation: We can write any whole number as a fraction over 1.

3. Answer: C
Explanation: Each whole is divided into 4 parts, so we have 5 wholes. This means we have 20×4=80 parts, so we write $\frac{20}{4}$.

4. Answer: B
Explanation: Each whole is divided into 3 parts, so we have 21 wholes. This means we have 63×3=189 parts, so we write $\frac{63}{3}$.

5. Answer: C
Explanation: Each whole is divided into 6 parts, so we have 12 parts shaded which is 2 wholes. This means we have 6×2 = 12 parts, so we write $\frac{12}{6}$.

6. Answer: D
Explanation: Each whole is divided into 4 parts, so we have 8 parts and 2 wholes. This means we have 4×2=8 parts, so we write $\frac{8}{4}$.

7. Answer: D
Explanation: Each whole is divided into 6 parts, so we have 6 wholes. This means we have 6×6=36 parts, so we write $\frac{36}{6}$.

8. Answer: A
Explanation: Each whole is divided into 4 parts, so we have 5 wholes. This means we have 5×4=20 parts, so we write $\frac{20}{4}$.

9. Answer: C
Explanation: Each whole is divided into 12 parts, so we have 6 wholes. This means we have 6×12=72 parts, so we write $\frac{72}{12}$.

10. Answer: A
Explanation: Each whole is divided into 9 parts, So we have 15 wholes. This means we have 9×15=135 parts, so we write $\frac{135}{5}$.

11. Answer: B
Explanation: Each whole is divided into 14 parts, so we have 5 wholes. This means we have 5×14=70 parts, so we write $\frac{70}{5}$.

12. Answer: D
Explanation: Each whole is divided into 12 parts, so we have 4 wholes. This means we have 12×4=48 parts, so we write $\frac{48}{12}$.

13. Answer: B
Explanation: Each whole is divided into 6 parts, so we have 5 wholes. This means we have 6×5=30 parts, so we write $\frac{30}{5}$.

14. Answer: D
Explanation: Each whole is divided into 10 parts, so we have 1 wholes. This means we have 10×1=10 parts, so we write $\frac{10}{1}$.

15. Answer: B
Explanation: Each whole is divided into 4 parts, so we have 4 wholes. This means we have 4×4=16 parts, so we write $\frac{16}{4}$.

16. Answer: C
Explanation: Each whole is divided into 10 parts, so we have 4 wholes. This means we have 10×4=40 parts, so we write $\frac{40}{4}$.

17. Answer: A
Explanation: Each whole is divided into 9 parts, so we have 9 wholes. This means we have 9×9=81 parts, so we write $\frac{81}{9}$.

18. Answer: D
Explanation: Each whole is divided into 3 parts, so we have 3 wholes. This means we have 3×3=9 parts, so we write $\frac{9}{3}$.

19. Answer: A
Explanation: Each whole is divided into 10 parts, so we have 5 wholes. This means we have 5×10=50 parts, so we write $\frac{50}{10}$.

20. Answer: $\frac{29}{1}$
Explanation:
We can write any whole number as a fraction over 1.

4.5 COMPARE THE FRACTIONS

1. Answer: $\frac{8}{9}$ > $\frac{8}{11}$
Explanation: If two fractions have the same numerator, the fraction with the smaller denominator is bigger.

2. Answer: $\frac{12}{7}$ < $\frac{12}{6}$
Explanation: If two fractions have the same numerator, the fraction with the smaller denominator is bigger.

3. Answer: $\frac{5}{4}$ < $\frac{6}{4}$
Explanation: If two fractions have the same denominator, the fraction with the larger numerator is bigger.

4. Answer: $\frac{13}{7}$ > $\frac{11}{7}$
Explanation: If two fractions have the same denominator, the fraction with the larger numerator is bigger.

5. Answer: $\frac{15}{9}$ = $\frac{15}{9}$
Explanation: If two fractions have the same denominator, and numerator they are equal.

6. Answer: B
Explanation: If two fractions have the numerator, the fraction with the smaller denominator is bigger.

7. Answer: B
Explanation: If two fractions have the same denominator, the fraction with the larger numerator is bigger.

8. Answer: B
Explanation: If two fractions have the numerator, the fraction with the smaller denominator is bigger.

9. Answer: A
Explanation: $\frac{4}{8} > \frac{3}{8}$, If two fractions have the same denominator, the fraction with the larger numerator is bigger.

10. Answer: A
Explanation: $\frac{7}{4} > \frac{7}{9}$, If two fractions have the numerator, the fraction with the smaller denominator is bigger.

11. Answer: B
Explanation: $\frac{5}{7} > \frac{5}{8}$, If two fractions have the numerator, the fraction with the smaller denominator is bigger.

12. Answer: A
Explanation: $\frac{9}{8} > \frac{6}{8}$, If two fractions have the same denominator, the fraction with the larger numerator is bigger.

13. Answer: A
Explanation: $\frac{4}{15} > \frac{4}{19}$, If two fractions have the same numerator, the fraction with the smaller denominator is bigger.

14. Answer: A
Explanation: $\frac{12}{9} < \frac{10}{9}$, If two fractions have the same denominator, the fraction with the larger numerator is bigger.

15. Answer: $\frac{35}{14} > \frac{30}{14}$
Explanation: If two fractions have the same denominator, the fraction with the larger numerator is bigger.

16. Answer: $\frac{11}{9} < \frac{11}{5}$
Explanation: If two fractions have the same numerator, the fraction with the smaller denominator is bigger.

17. Answer: A
Explanation: $\frac{4}{2} < \frac{4}{5}$, If two fractions have the same numerator, the fraction with the smaller denominator is bigger.

18. Answer: A
Explanation: If two fractions have the numerator, the fraction with the smaller denominator is bigger.

19. Answer: A
Explanation: If two fractions have the same denominator, the fraction with the larger numerator is bigger.

20. Answer: B
Explanation: If two fractions have the same denominator, and numerator they are equal.

4.6 CHAPTER REVIEW

1. Answer: D
Explanation: The denominator is the bottom number of the fraction's and the number of parts into which the whole was split.

2. Answer: C
Explanation: The numerator is the top number of the fraction's and the number of pieces of the whole we have.

3. Answer: A
Explanation: There are 5 squares, and 2 are shaded.

4. Answer: C
Explanation: We write the number of damaged carrots(the number of parts we have) over the total number of carrots (parts of the whole).

ANSWERS AND EXPLANATIONS

5. Answer: D
Explanation: $\frac{5\times2}{9\times2} = \frac{10}{18}$.

6. Answer: B
Explanation: We write the number of books checked out (the number of parts we have) over the total number of books (total number of parts).

7. Answer: C
Explanation: We write the number of rotten dates (the number of parts we have) over the total number of dates (total number of parts).

8. Answer: B
Explanation: We write the number of kids with black bags (the number of parts we have) over the total number of kids (total number of parts).

9. Answer: B
Explanation: We write the number of Pizzas sold (the number of parts we have) over the total number of pizzas (total number of parts).

10. Answer: A
Explanation: We write the number of rotten watermelons (the number of parts we have) over the total number of watermelons (the total number of parts).

11. Answer: C
Explanation: Remaining all options are equivalent to $\frac{6}{7}$
Only $\frac{6}{7} \neq \frac{12}{7}$.

12.Answer: C
Explanation: $\frac{4\times2}{9\times2} = \frac{8}{18}$.

13. Answer: B
Explanation: $\frac{6}{5} \neq \frac{12}{14}$.

14. Answer: B
Explanation: $\frac{3}{15} = \frac{6}{x}$, $\frac{3\times2}{15\times2} = \frac{6}{30}$.

15. Answer: A
Explanation: $\frac{5}{6} = \frac{15}{18}$.

16. Answer: A
Explanation: We can write any whole number as a fraction over 1.

17. Answer: C
Explanation: Each whole is divided into 5 parts and we have 13 wholes. This means we have 65×5=325 parts, so we write $\frac{65}{5}$.

18. Answer: D
Explanation: Each whole is divided into 12 parts and we have 4 wholes. This means we have 3×4=12 parts, so we write $\frac{12}{3}$.

19. Answer: A
Explanation: Each whole is divided into 10 parts and we have 5 wholes. This means we have 5×10=50 parts, so we write $\frac{50}{10}$.

20. Answer: A
Explanation: Each whole is divided into 3 parts and we have 7 wholes. This means we have 3×7=21 parts, so we write $\frac{21}{7}$.

5. MEASUREMENT

5.1 TIME INTERVALS TO THE NEAREST MINUTE

1. Answer: A
Explanation: To find the hours, look before the: sign, and to find the minutes look after the: sign.

2. Answer: C
Explanation: The hour hand points between 12 and 1. It shows 1 hour. Next read the minute. Start at the 12. Count by 5s until you reach the minute hand.
The minute hand shows 45 minutes.

3. Answer: B
Explanation: To find the hours, look before the: sign, and to find the minutes look after the: sign.

4. Answer: A
Explanation: Since Lisa must wake up in the morning to complete homework and to go to school, the time must be 6 A.M.

5. Answer: D
Explanation: Subtract hours = 6 − 0 = 6
Subtract minutes = 50 − 5 = 45
Combine: 6:45.

6. Answer: C
Explanation: The hour hand points between 10 and 11. It shows 10 hour. Next read the minutes. Start at the 12. Count by 5s until you reach the minute hand. The minute hand shows 38 minutes.

7. Answer: A
Explanation: Add hours = 10 + 0 = 10
Add minutes = 45 + 45 = 90 => 90 − 60 = 30
Add 1 to hours = 10 + 1 = 11. Combine: 11:30.

8. Answer: B
Explanation: Add hours = 1 + 0 = 1
Add minutes = 56 + 35 = 91 => 91 − 60 = 31
Add 1 to hours = 1 + 1 = 2. Combine: 2:31.

9. Answer: C
Explanation: Add hours = 8 + 0 = 8
Add minutes = 23 + 25 = 48. Combine: 8:48.

10. Answer: 3:37
Explanation: Add hours = 3 + 0 = 3
Add minutes = 0 + 37 = 37. Combine: 3:37.

11. Answer: D
Explanation: The timeline indicates a time 6:15. The short hand of the analog clock is between the 6 and 7 and the long hand is pointing 15 which matches the timeline.

12. Answer: B
Explanation: Subtract hours = 12 − 8 = 4
Subtract minutes = 12 − 46 = − 34 =>
−34 + 60 = 26; Subtract 1 to hours = 4 − 1 = 3.
Combine: 3:26.

13. Answer: D
Explanation: Subtract hours = 7 − 2 = 5
Subtract minutes = 54 − 9 = 45
Subtract 1 to hours = 5 − 1 = 4. Combine: 4:45.

14. Answer: 03:45
Explanation: Add hours = 2 + 0 = 2
Add minutes = 44 + 21 = 65 => 65 − 60 = 5
Add 1 to hours = 2 + 1 = 3. Combine: 03:05.

15. Answer: C
Explanation: Add hours = 10 + 0 = 10
Add minutes = 40 + 55 = 95 => 95 − 60 = 35
Add 1 to hours = 10 + 1 = 11. Combine: 11:35.

16. Answer: B
Explanation: Add hours = 5 + 2 = 7
Add minutes = 20 + 13 = 33. Combine: 07:33.

17. Answer: A
Explanation: Add hours = 3 + 5 = 8
Add minutes = 30 + 0 = 30. Combine: 08:30.

18. Answer: 02:37
Explanation: Add hours = 12 + 2 = 14 =>
14 − 12 = 2 (Remember we are using a 12 hours clock),
Add minutes = 27 + 10 = 37. Combine: 02:37.

19. Answer: C
Explanation: Add hours = 8 + 4 = 12
Add minutes = 51 + 10 = 61 => 61 − 60 = 1
Add 1 to hours = 12 + 1 = 13 =>
13 − 12 = 1 (Remember we are using a 12 hours clock) Combine: 01:01.

20. Answer: A
Explanation: Subtract hours = 2 − 1 = 1
Subtract minutes = 37 − 17 = 20.
Combine: 01:20.

5.2 ESTIMATE LIQUID VOLUMES AND MASSES

1. Answer: D
Explanation: Buses have a large mass, so we measure them in kilograms.

2. Answer: C
Explanation: A pen is an item with a small mass, so we measure it in grams.

3. Answer: D
Explanation: A raindrop holds very little, so we measure the volume in milliliters.

4. Answer: A
Explanation: A barrel holds a large amount, so we measure the volume in liters.

5. Answer: B
Explanation: A tall juice glass holds approximately 350 ml. 2 ml is much too little. 10 g is not a measure of volume. 1 L is much too large for a drinking glass.

6. Answer: C
Explanation: A toothbrush is not an object with a large mass. Therefore, 18 g is a reasonable approximation. 1 kg is much too large. 45 ml and 3 L are not a measures of mass.

7. Answer: B
Explanation: Because apples and oranges are high-mass items so we measure them in kilograms.

8. Answer: A
Explanation: A tank has a large capacity so we measure it in liters.

9. Answer: C
Explanation: A white rose is an item with a small mass, so we measure it in grams.

10. Answer: D
Explanation: 5 packs of sugar have a large mass so we measure them in kilograms.

11. Answer: A
Explanation: A ring is an item with a small mass, so we measure it in grams.

12. Answer: C
Explanation: An oil can have a large capacity so we measure it in liters.

13. Answer: B
Explanation: The school van has a large mass, so we measure it in kilograms.

14. Answer: D
Explanation: The watermelon has a large mass so we measure them in kilograms.

15. Answer: 2 grams
Explanation: A paper sheet has a small mass, so we measure it in grams.

16. Answer: C
Explanation: A large bucket has a large capacity so we measure it in liters.

17. Answer: B
Explanation: A coffee cup holds very little so we measure the volume in milliliters.

18. Answer: B
Explanation: The water glass holds approximately 250 ml. 3 ml is much too little. 50 g is not a measure of volume. 7 L is much too large for a drinking glass.

19. Answer: C
Explanation: A small stone is not an object with a large mass. Therefore 7 g is a reasonable approximation. 4 kg is much too large. 15 ml and 2 L are not a measure of mass.

20. Answer: A
Explanation: A smartphone has a small mass, so we measure it in grams.

5.3 ADD AND SUBTRACT INVOLVING MASSES OR VOLUMES

1. Answer: B
Explanation: 255 + 173 = 200 + 50 + 5 + 100 + 70 + 3 = 300 + 120 + 8 = 428.

2. Answer: C
Explanation: 13 + 16 + 19 = 10 + 3 + 10 + 6 + 10 + 9 = 30 + 18 = 48.

3. Answer: A
Explanation: 893 + 97 = 800 + 90 + 3 + 90 + 7 = 800 + 180 + 10 = 990 liters.

4. Answer: C
Explanation: 510 - 457 = 500 + 10 + 0 - 400 - 50 - 7 = 53 ml.

5. Answer: D
Explanation: 188 + 126 = 100 + 80 + 8 + 100 + 20 + 6 = 200 + 100 + 14 = 314 kg.

6. Answer: C
Explanation: 312 + 157 = 300 + 10 + 2 + 100 + 50 + 7 = 400 + 60 + 9 = 469 ml.

7. Answer: B
Explanation: 78 - 21 = 70 + 8 - 20 - 1 = 57 kg.

8. Answer: D
Explanation: 63 - 22 = 60 + 3 - 20 - 2 = 41 L.

9. Answer: A
Explanation: 432 + 486 = 400 + 30 + 2 + 400 + 80 + 6 = 918 grams.

10. Answer: C
Explanation: 543 - 398 = 500 + 40 + 3 - 300 - 90 - 8 = 145 L.

11. Answer: 102 kg
Explanation: 55 + 47 = 50+5+40+7 = 102 kg.

12. Answer: 682 kg
Explanation:
939-257=900+30+9-200-50-7=682 kg

13. Answer: B
Explanation: 750-500=700+50-500=250 grams

14. Answer: D
Explanation:
491+377=400+90+1+300+70+7=868 kg

15. Answer: A
Explanation:
255-115=200+50+5-100-10-5=140 grams

16. Answer: C
Explanation: 76+87=70+6+80+7 = 163 kg.

17. Answer: 434 ml
Explanation:
758-324=700+50+8-300-20-4 = 434 ml.

18. Answer: 587 kg
Explanation:
876-289=800+70+6-200-80-9 = 587 kg.

19. Answer: B
Explanation:
574+371=500+70+4+300+70+1 = 945 L.

20. Answer: C
Explanation:
956-250=900+50+6-200-50 = 706 ml.

5.4 MULTIPLY AND DIVIDE INVOLVING MASSES AND VOLUMES

1. Answer: A
Explanation: 27 × 7 = 189 ml.

2. Answer: C
Explanation: 70 g × 10 = 700 g.

3. Answer: B
Explanation: 88 kg ÷ 8 = 11 kg.

4. Answer: A
Explanation: Amos has 108 L milk.
He divides into 9 containers. 108 ÷ 9 = 12 L.

5. Answer: C
Explanation: Number of slices of pizza Roy buy = 6. One pizza weighs = 90 grams
$6 \times 90 = 6 \times (9 \times 10) = (6 \times 9) \times 10 = 54 \times 10 = 540$ g.

6. Answer: D
Explanation: Total amount of cake = 10 kg
He divided it into 10 parts. $10 \div 10 = 1$ kg.

7. Answer: B
Explanation: Total amount of tomato =3 kg
Total amount of potato =5 kg. $3 \times 5 = 15$ kg.

8. Answer: A
Explanation: Bella serves French fries = 5 guests. One guest = 70 g of French fries
$5 \times 70 = 5 \times (7 \times 10) = (5 \times 7) \times 10 = 350$ g.

9. Answer: C
Explanation: Total number of bags Aurora has =3. Total mass of 3 bags =90 kg
Mass of one bag $=90 \div 3 = (9 \times 10) \div 3 = (9 \div 3) \times 10 = 3 \times 10 = 30$ kg.

10. Answer: D
Explanation: Number of jugs Elvis carries =8
One jug contains water =2 L. 8 jugs=$8 \times 2 = 16$ L.

11. Answer: 40 ml
Explanation: Number of travel shampoo packets Randy has = 4.
One travel shampoo packet contains = 10 ml.
4 travel shampoo packets =$4 \times 10 = 40$ ml.

12. Answer: 480 g
Explanation: Mass of one chocolate =80 g
Mass of 6 chocolates = $6 \times 80 = 6 \times (8 \times 10) = (6 \times 8) \times 10 = 480$ g.

13. Answer: 30 L
Explanation: Total amount of orange juice =150 L. $150 \div 5 = 30$ L.

14. Answer: A
Explanation: $400 \div 40 = (40 \times 10) \div (4 \times 10) = 40 \div 4 = 10$ml.

15. Answer: B
Explanation: $9 \times 11 = 99$ kg.

16. Answer: C
Explanation:
$750 \div 250 = (75 \times 10) \div (25 \times 10) = 75 \div 25 = 3$.

17. Answer: D
Explanation: $500 \div 4 = 125$ g.

18. Answer: B
Explanation: $81 \div 9 = 9$.

19. Answer: A
Explanation: Number of books in bag =8
One book = 2 kg
Eight books = $8 \times 2 = 16$ kg.

20. Answer: C
Explanation: $27 \div 1 = 27$.

5.5 REPRESENT AND INTERPRET DATA

1. Answer: B
Explanation: The values in the table do not correspond to the values represented by the bar graph.

2. Answer: A
Explanation: The values in the table correspond to the values represented by the bar graph.

3. Answer: A
Explanation: The values in the table correspond to the values represented by the line graph.

4. Answer: B
Explanation: The values in the table do not correspond to the values represented by the line graph.

5. Answer: C
Explanation: The height of the bars in the graph corresponds to the values presented in the table.

6. Answer: D
Explanation: The height of the bars in the graph correspond to the values presented in the table.

7. Answer: A
Explanation: The points on the line graph correspond to the values presented in the table.

8. Answer: C
Explanation: The points on the line graph correspond to the values presented in the table.

9. Answer: B
Explanation: The height of the bar corresponding to Hot dogs is 7.

10. Answer: D
Explanation: Number of mulberry trees = 20
Number of Plum trees = 15. 20-15 = 5.

11. Answer: A
Explanation: Number of Almond joy = 28
Number of Butterfinger = 16. 28+16 = 44.

12. Answer: C
Explanation: Total number of crayons = 24
Total number of pens = 28.
$24+ \frac{1}{4}(28) = 24+7 = 31$.

13. Answer: B
Explanation: Number of shirt = 8
Number of skirt = 9. Number of T-shirt = 11
8 + 9 + 11 = 28.

14. Answer: C
Explanation: The left edge of the rectangle is aligned with the edge of the ruler, and it ends at the $5\frac{1}{4}$ inch mark on the ruler.

15. Answer: B
Explanation: The left edge of the rectangle is aligned with the edge of the ruler, and it ends at the $8\frac{1}{2}$ inch mark on the ruler.

16. Answer: D
Explanation: $7\frac{1}{2} -1\frac{1}{2} = 6$.

17. Answer: A
Explanation: $9\frac{1}{4} - \frac{3}{4} = 8\frac{1}{2}$.

18. Answer: $5\frac{1}{2}$
Explanation:
$$8\frac{1}{2} -3=5\frac{1}{2}$$

19. Answer: $3\frac{1}{2}$
Explanation: $8\frac{3}{4} -5\frac{1}{4} =3\frac{2}{4} =3\frac{1}{2}$.

20. Answer: $9\frac{3}{4}$
Explanation:
The tree is aligned with the left edge of the ruler and the cherries are at the $9\frac{3}{4}$ inch marker.

5.6 CHAPTER REVIEW

---

1. Answer: B
Explanation: A bottle of lavender essential oil is small, use milliliter.

2. Answer: C
Explanation: The cylinder shape starts at 0 inches and ends at 4 inches on the ruler. The length is 4 inches.

3. Answer: D
Explanation: The shorter hand is the hour hand. It points to the 7. The longer hand is the minute hand. It points to the space between 9 and 10 (approximately 47 minutes after 7).

4. Answer: B
Explanation: The sofa starts at 0 and ends at $7\frac{3}{4}$ on the ruler. The length is $7\frac{3}{4}$.

5. Answer: C
Explanation: Grams are used for the mass of the men's running shoes.

6. Answer: A
Explanation: The line segment starts at 2 and ends at $7\frac{1}{4}$ on the ruler. The length is $5\frac{1}{4}$.

7. Answer: A
Explanation: The shorter hand is the hour hand and the longer hand is the minute hand. The hour hand is pointing between 3 and 4 the minute hand points between 4 and 5. It is 3:23.

8. Answer: 12:10
Explanation: Add hours = 8+3 = 11
Add minutes = 53+17 = 70 => 70-60 = 10
Add 1 to hours = 11+1 = 12. Combine: 12:10.

9. Answer: 6:55
Explanation: Add hours = 4+2 = 6
Add minutes = 35+20 = 55. Combine: 6:55.

10. Answer: 3:07
Explanation: Subtract hours = 7-4 = 3
Subtract minutes = 54-47 = 7. Combine: 3:07.

11. Answer: A
Explanation: 403+312 = 400+3+300+10+2 = 700+10+5 = 715 grams.

12. Answer: C
Explanation:
749-299 = 700+40+9-200-90-9 = 450 L.

13. Answer: B
Explanation: 8×9 =72 ml.

14. Answer: D
Explanation: 7×2 = 14 kg.

15. Answer: B
Explanation: 93÷3 = 31.

16. Answer: C
Explanation: The timeline indicates a time 8:30. The short hand of the analog clock is between 8 and 9 and the long hand is pointing 30 which matches the timeline.

17. Answer: A
Explanation: Subtract hours = 10-5 = 5
Subtract minutes = 43-39 = 4. Combine: 5:04

18. Answer: A
Explanation: The values in the table correspond to the values represented by the line graph.

19. Answer: D
Explanation: Number of black color shoes =19
Number of blue color shoes =9. 19-9=10.

20. Answer: B
Explanation: $6\frac{1}{4} - 1\frac{1}{4}$ =5 inches.

6. GEOMETRIC MEASUREMENT

6.1 AREA OF SQUARES, RECTANGLES, AND RECTILINEAR FIGURES

1.Answer: B
Explanation:

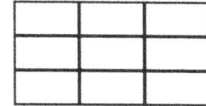

There are 9 squares in the rectangle.

2. Answer: D
Explanation:

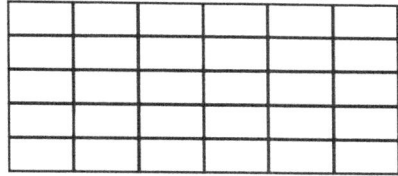

There are 30 squares in the rectangle.

3. Answer: A
Explanation: There are 8 squares in the rectangle.

4. Answer: B
Explanation:

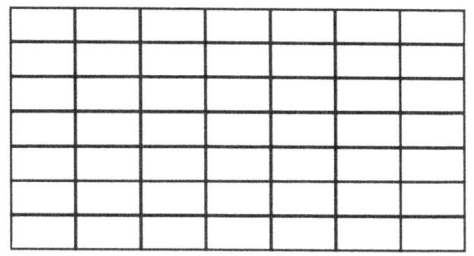

There are 49 squares in the rectangle.

5. Answer: C
Explanation:
There are 5 squares in the rectangle.

6. Answer: A
Explanation: $7 \times (3+3) = 42$.

7. Answer: A
Explanation: $3 \times (3+1) = 12$.

8. Answer: B
Explanation: $10 \times 2 + 10 \times 2 = 20+20 = 40$.

9. Answer: 117
Explanation: $9 \times 7 + 9 \times 6 = 63+54 = 117$.

10. Answer: 275
Explanation: $10 \times 11 + 15 \times 11 = 110+165 = 275$.

11. Answer: 28
Explanation: $6 \times 5 - 1 \times 2 = 30-2 = 28$.

12. Answer: 100
Explanation: $8 \times 10 + 4 \times 5 = 80+20 = 100$.

13. Answer: 210
Explanation: $30 \times 9 - 12 \times 5 = 270-60 = 210$.

14. Answer: 191
Explanation: $15 \times 17 - 4 \times 4 - 4 \times 4 - 4 \times 4 - 4 \times 4 = 255-16-16-16-16 = 191$.

15. Answer: 86
Explanation: $4 \times 8 + 3 \times 9 + 3 \times 9 = 32+27+27 = 86$.

16. Answer: A
Explanation: There are 2 squares in the rectangle.

17. Answer: A
Explanation: $3 \times 4 + 8 \times 2 = 12+16 = 28$.

18. Answer: B
Explanation: $4 \times 6 - 2 \times 3 = 24-6 = 18$.

19. Answer: A
Explanation: There are 20 squares in the rectangle.

20. Answer: B
Explanation:

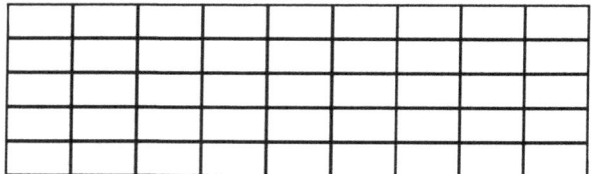

There are 45 squares in the rectangle.

6.2 PERIMETER GIVEN SIDE LENGTH

1. Answer: C
Explanation:
25+25+36+36 = 20+5+20+5+36+36 = 122.

2. Answer: D
Explanation: 89+89+55+55 =
80+9+80+9+50+5+50+5 = 288.

3. Answer: C
Explanation:
63+63+17+17 = 60+3+60+3+10+7+10+7 = 160.

4. Answer: A
Explanation:
95+95+29 = 90+5+90+5+20+9 = 219.

5. Answer: A
Explanation:
70+70+50 = 60+10+60+10+20+20 = 190.

6. Answer: B
Explanation: 89+89+42+42 =
80+9+80+9+40+2+40+2 = 262.

7. Answer: A
Explanation: 120+120+75+75 =
100+20+100+20+70+5+70+5 = 390.

8. Answer: B
Explanation: 30+71+48+80+25 =
30+70+1+40+8+80+20+5 = 254.

9. Answer: C
Explanation:
20+20+20+20 = 20×4 = 10×2+10×2 = 80.

10. Answer: B
Explanation: 69+69+95+95 =
60+9+60+9+90+5+90+5 = 138+190 = 328.

11. Answer: A
Explanation: 15+15+22+22 =
10+5+10+5+20+2+20+2 = 30+44 = 74.

12. Answer: D
Explanation: 25+37+55+49+11 =
20+5+30+7+50+5+40+9+10+1 = 117+60 = 177.

13. Answer: A
Explanation: 29+47+65+59+31 =
20+9+40+7+60+5+50+9+30+1 = 200+31 = 231.

14. Answer: B
Explanation: 39+46+52+11+71+30 =
30+9+40+6+50+2+10+1+70+1+30 = 249.

15. Answer: D
Explanation: 750+750+890 =
700+50+700+50+800+90 = 1500+890 = 2390.

16. Answer: D
Explanation: 390+469+743 =
300+90+460+9+740+3 = 859+743 = 1602.

17. Answer: A
Explanation: 77+52+40+33+64 =
70+7+50+2+40+30+3+60+4 = 266.

18. Answer: C
Explanation: 90+90+52+52 =
80+10+80+10+50+2+50+2 = 180+104 = 284.

19. Answer: D
Explanation: 57+57+40+40 =
50+7+50+7+20+20+20+20 = 114+80 = 194.

20. Answer: A
Explanation: 29+82+31+95 =
20+9+80+2+30+1+90+5 = 111+126 = 237.

6.3 PERIMETER OF POLYGON

1. Answer: B
Explanation:
$155+155+155 = 155 \times 3 = 100 \times 3 + 55 \times 3 = 465$.

2. Answer: D
Explanation: $175+148+205 = 100+75+100+48+200+5 = 323+205 = 528$.

3. Answer: A
Explanation: $99+99+99+99+99+99+99 = 99 \times 7 = 90 \times 7 + 9 \times 7 = 630+63 = 693$.

4. Answer: D
Explanation:
$57+57+39+39+78+78 = 153+195 = 348$.

5. Answer: B
Explanation: $15+15+32+32 = 30+64 = 94$.

6. Answer: C
Explanation: $85+85+85+85+85+85+85+85+85+85+85 = 85 \times 12 = 80 \times 12 + 5 \times 12 = 960+60 = 1020$.

7. Answer: A
Explanation: $215+25+120+145+38+255+180 = 200+15+20+5+100+20+140+5+30+8+250+5+100+80 = 978$.

8. Answer: B
Explanation: $115+147+125+159+131 = 100+15+140+7+120+5+150+9+100+31 = 677$.

9. Answer: C
Explanation:
$140+140+105+105 = 280+210 = 490$.

10. Answer: A
Explanation:
$250+250+82+82 = 500+164 = 664$.

11. Answer: A
Explanation: A square has four sides, $60 \div 4 = 15$.

12. Answer: B
Explanation: A square has four sides, $16 \div 4 = 4$.

13. Answer: B
Explanation: A rectangle has four sides, The lengths of 3 sides of the rectangle are 135 mm, 135 mm, and 80 mm and the Perimeter is 430 mm. $430-135-135-80 = 400+30-100-35-100-35-80 = 80$.

14. Answer: A
Explanation: A trapezoid has four sides, The lengths of 3 sides of the rectangle are 55 mm, 125 mm, and 125 mm and the Perimeter is 360 mm. $360-55-125-125 = 300+60-50-5-100-25-100-25 = 55$.

15. Answer: C
Explanation: An equilateral octagon has eight sides, $128 \div 8 = 16$.

16. Answer: C
Explanation: An equilateral decagon has ten sides, $270 \div 10 = 27$.

17. Answer: A
Explanation: An equilateral pentagon has five sides, $115 \div 5 = 23$.

18. Answer: D
Explanation: A rectangle has four sides, The lengths of 3 sides of the rectangle are 65 cm, 90 cm, and 95 cm, and the Perimeter is 315 mm.
$315-65-90-95 = 300+15-60+5-90-90-5 = 65$.

19. Answer: C
Explanation: A square has four sides, $180 \div 4 = 45$.

20. Answer: B
Explanation: An equilateral triangle has three sides, $225 \div 3 = 75$.

6.4 RECTANGLES WITH THE PERIMETER AND AREAS

1. Answer: C
Explanation: 2×8 = 16.

2. Answer: D
Explanation: 2+2+8+8 = 20.

3. Answer: C
Explanation: 12×22 = 264.

4. Answer: C
Explanation: 12+12+22+22 = 68.

5. Answer: D
Explanation: 5×15 = 75 = 3×25.

6. Answer: A
Explanation: 3×66 = 198 = 33×6.

7. Answer: C
Explanation: 5+5+14+14 = 38 = 10+10+9+9.

8. Answer: B
Explanation: 6+6+12+12 = 36 = 15+15+3+3.

9. Answer: B
Explanation: 16+16+30+30 = 92 = 22+22+24+24.

10. Answer: D
Explanation: 15×35 = 525 = 25×21.

11. Answer: A
Explanation: 8+8+8+8 = 32.

12. Answer: C
Explanation: 88÷11 = 8.

13. Answer: B
Explanation: Width: 70-15-15 = 40÷2 = 20
Area: 15×20 = 300.

14. Answer: C
Explanation: 90-16-16 = 58÷2 = 29.

15. Answer: A
Explanation: Width: 120-25-25 = 70÷2 = 35
Area: 35×25 = 875.

16. Answer: A
Explanation: 250÷10 = 25.

17. Answer: C
Explanation: Width: 120÷8 = 15
Perimeter: 8+8+15+15 = 46

18. Answer: B
Explanation: Width: 225÷15 = 15
Perimeter: 15+15+15+15 = 60.

19. Answer: B
Explanation: Width: 144-36-36 = 72÷2 = 36
Area: 36×36 = 1296.

20. Answer: B
Explanation: 18×23 = 414.

6.5 CHAPTER REVIEW

1. Answer: A
Explanation:

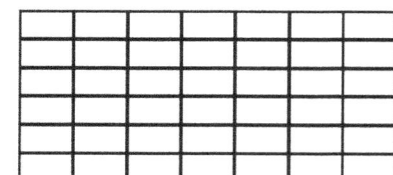

There are 42 squares in the rectangle.

2. Answer: D
Explanation: There are 12 squares in the rectangle.

3. Answer: C
Explanation: 4×(4+4) = 32.

4. Answer: C
Explanation: 15×20+12×10 = 300+120 = 420.

5. Answer: A
Explanation: There are 40 squares in the rectangle.

6. Answer: B
Explanation: 75+75+27+27 =
70+5+70+5+20+7+20+7 = 204.

7. Answer: C
Explanation: 35+78+68+92+27 =
30+5+70+8+60+8+90+2+20+7 = 300.

8. Answer: A
Explanation:
80+80+55 = 70+10+70+10+50+5 = 215.

9. Answer: B
Explanation: 82+82+30+30 =
80+2+80+2+20+10+20+10 = 224.

10. Answer: C
Explanation: 40+40+15+15 = 110.

11. Answer: B
Explanation:
120+120+120 = 120×3 = 100×3+20×3 = 360.

12. Answer: C
Explanation: 25+25+25+25+25+25+25 = 25×7
= 20×7+5×7 = 140+35 = 175.

13. Answer: C
Explanation: A square has four sides,
160÷4 = 40.

14. Answer: B
Explanation: A rectangle has four sides, The lengths of 3 sides of the rectangle are 55 mm, 55 mm, and 20 mm and the Perimeter is 430 mm.
150-55-55-20 = 100+50-50-5-50-5-20 = 20.

15. Answer: B
Explanation: An equilateral octagon has eight sides, 440÷8 = 55.

16. Answer: A
Explanation: An equilateral decagon has ten sides, 650÷10 = 65.

17. Answer: B
Explanation: 30+30+45+45 = 150.

18. Answer: D
Explanation: 90÷10 = 9.

19. Answer: C
Explanation: Width: 220-20-20 = 180÷2 = 90
Area: 90×20 = 1800.

20. Answer: C
Explanation: 110-15-15 = 80÷2 = 40 .

7. SHAPES

7.1 UNDERSTANDING ATTRIBUTES OF SHAPES

1. Answer: C
Explanation: It has 4 equal sides but stands on a vertex.

2. Answer: A
Explanation: Two sides of a shape are parallel if lines placed along them never cross.

3. Answer: B
Explanation: A hexagon has 6 sides.

4. Answer: D
Explanation: A pentagon has 5 sides.

5. Answer: B
Explanation: The sides have different lengths.

6. Answer: A
Explanation: A rectangle has 2 pairs of opposite sides that are equal and parallel.

7. Answer: C
Explanation: All sides are a different length and all angles are a different measure. This describes a scalene triangle.

ANSWERS AND EXPLANATIONS

8. Answer: D
Explanation: A square has 4 sides of equal length and 4 right angles.

9. Answer: A
Explanation: All the sides are the same length.

10. Answer: B
Explanation: Two sides of a shape are parallel if lines placed along them never cross.

11. Answer: C
Explanation: A quadrilateral is a polygon with four sides. So, a square is a quadrilateral.

12. Answer: 4
Explanation: Vertex is a point where two straight lines or edges intersect. A quadrilateral has 4 vertices.

13. Answer: A
Explanation: A kite has two pairs of adjacent, congruent sides.

14. Answer: B
Explanation: If the lengths of the sides are not equal, then the shape is irregular shape.

15. Answer: B
Explanation: They are all parallelograms. Each figure has a pair of parallel sides.

16. Answer: C
Explanation: An Octagon is an 8-sided polygon.

17. Answer: A
Explanation: A trapezoid can have a right angle, but to be a trapezoid it must have exactly one pair of parallel lines.

18. Answer: C
Explanation: A rectangle has four right angles and two opposites, congruent, parallel lines.

19. Answer: B
Explanation: A heptagon has 7 sides.

20. Answer: D
Explanation: A kite has two sets of adjacent, equal-length sides.

7.2 QUADRILATERALS AND NON-QUADRILATERAL

1. Answer: A
Explanation: A kite has two sets of adjacent, congruent sides.

2. Answer: B
Explanation: A rhombus is made up of 4 congruent sides.

3. Answer: C
Explanation: A trapezoid has exactly one pair of parallel lines.

4. Answer: D
Explanation: A quadrilateral is a polygon with four sides.

5. Answer: A
Explanation: A square has 4 equal sides and a rectangle has two pairs of opposite, congruent sides.

6. Answer: B
Explanation: A quadrilateral has 4 sides. So, the statement is false.

7. Answer: C
Explanation: A rhombus has 4 equal-length sides.

8. Answer: D
Explanation: A quadrilateral is a polygon with 4 sides.

9. Answer: B
Explanation: A quadrilateral has 4 sides.

10. Answer: A
Explanation: A rectangle has two pairs of opposite, congruent sides.

11. Answer: C
Explanation: A rectangle has 4 right angles.

12. Answer: D
Explanation: A kite is a quadrilateral with two distinct pairs of equal adjacent sides.

13. Answer: B
Explanation: Count the sides of both shapes.

14. Answer: A
Explanation: A square has 4 right angles. There is no strict definition of the measurement of the angles of a rhombus.

15. Answer: James is incorrect
Explanation: Every quadrilateral is not a parallelogram. A parallelogram is a quadrilateral with two pairs of parallel sides.

16. Answer: D
Explanation: A parallelogram has exact 2 sets of parallel lines.

17. Answer: B
Explanation: The polygon has 7 sides. Quadrilaterals have 4 sides.

18. Answer: B
Explanation: A rhombus is made up of two equal-length sets of parallel lines.

19. Answer: A
Explanation: Two sides of a shape are parallel if lines placed along them never cross.

20. Answer: A
Explanation: A quadrilateral has 4 sides.

1. Answer: A
Explanation: 1 out of 6 equal parts are shaded.

2. Answer: C
Explanation: 4 out of 5 equal parts are not shaded.

3. Answer: B
Explanation: There are 8 equal-sized slices and she takes 4 so we write $\frac{4}{8}$.

4. Answer: D
Explanation: 2 out of 5 equal parts are shaded.

5. Answer: A
Explanation: There are 6 equal parts and 5 are shaded, so it is $\frac{5}{6}$.

6. Answer: C
Explanation: 3 out of 7 equal parts are shaded, so it is $\frac{3}{7}$.

7. Answer: B
Explanation: 2 out of 4 equal parts are shaded, so it is $\frac{2}{4}$.

8. Answer: D
Explanation: There are 8 equal parts and $8 - 5 = 3$ are not shaded, so it is $\frac{3}{8}$.

9. Answer: A
Explanation: 4 out of 5 equal parts is shaded, so it is $\frac{4}{5}$.

10. Answer: B
Explanation: The first picture has fewer equal parts than the second picture, so the parts in the first picture are larger. More of the first picture is shaded.

11. Answer: C
Explanation: There are 10 fruits and 4 apples, so it is $\frac{4}{10}$.

12. Answer: $\frac{2}{6}$
Explanation: The model is divided into 6 equal areas. 2 shaded area represents $\frac{2}{6}$.

13. Answer: B
Explanation: 2 out of 5 equal parts are shaded, so it is $\frac{2}{5}$.

14. Answer: D
Explanation: 5 out of 8 equal parts are shaded, so it is $\frac{5}{8}$.

15. Answer: A
Explanation: There are 9 equal parts and $9 - 5 = 4$ are not shaded, so it is $\frac{4}{9}$.

16. Answer: B
Explanation: 7 out of 10 equal parts are shaded, so it is $\frac{5}{10}$. So it is false.

17. Answer: C
Explanation: 1 out of 4 equal parts are shaded, so it is $\frac{1}{4}$.

18. Answer: D
Explanation: 7 out of 12 bikes were sold in that week, so it is $\frac{7}{12}$.

19. Answer: $\frac{5}{7}$
Explanation: 5 out of 7 equal parts are shaded, so it is $\frac{5}{7}$.

20. Answer: D
Explanation: There are 6 equal parts and $6 - 1 = 5$ are not shaded, so it is $\frac{5}{6}$.

7.4 CHAPTER REVIEW

1. Answers: B
Explanation: The sides of the figure have different lengths, so it is irregular.

2. Answers: A
Explanation: The quadrilateral has exactly one set of parallel sides.

3. Answer: C
Explanation: A rhombus is a parallelogram with opposite equal acute angles, opposite equal obtuse angles, and four equal sides.

4. Answer: D
Explanation: A square has 4 equal sides and 4 right angles.

5. Answer: C
Explanation: A hexagon is a 6-sided polygon.

6. Answer: D
Explanation: 4 out of 10 equal parts are shaded, so it is $\frac{4}{10}$.

7. Answer: 3
Explanation: Vertex is a point where two straight lines or edges intersect. A triangle has three vertices.

8. Answer: A
Explanation: A hexagon has 6 sides.

9. Answer: B
Explanation: 1 out of 5 equal parts are shaded, so it is $\frac{1}{5}$.

10. Answer: D
Explanation: A quadrilateral has 4 sides.

11. Answer: C
Explanation: A parallelogram is a quadrilateral with two pairs of parallel sides.

12. Answer: D
Explanation: A pentagon has 5 sides.

13. Answer: A
Explanation: There are 6 equal parts and $6 - 2 = 4$ are not shaded, so it is $\frac{4}{6}$.

14. Answer: C
Explanation: A Trapezoid has exactly one pair of parallel lines.

15. Answer: B
Explanation: The polygon has 5 sides. Quadrilaterals have 4 sides.

16. Answer: D
Explanation: There are 9 equal sized parts and 4 are taken, so $\frac{4}{9}$.

17. Answer: C
Explanation: A parallelogram has 2 sets of parallel lines.

18. Answer: B
Explanation: There are 10 equal parts and $10 - 7 = 3$ are not shaded, so it is $\frac{3}{10}$. So it is false.

19. Answer: A
Explanation: Shape is a heptagon and has 7 sides. So, option D is correct.

20. Answer: C
Explanation: There are 8 equal parts and $8 - 5 = 3$ are not shaded, so it is $\frac{3}{8}$.

COMPREHENSIVE ASSESSMENT 1

1. Answer: B
Explanation: 24 shells split into 4 bags is the same as $24 \div 4 = n$. Use the related multiplication equation to solve for the unknown factor: $4 \times n = 24$, $4 \times 6 = 24$, $24 \div 4 = 6$ so the unknown factor is 6. There are 6 shells in each bag.

2. Answer: B
Explanation: $30 \div 5 = 6$ matches the diagram because the total amount represented is 30 which is divided into 5 groups, with 6 in each group.

3. Answer: A
Explanation: Mrs. Logan has 40 pieces of candy in total. She uses 5 pieces in each bag, so think 40 pieces divided by 5 in a group = how many groups? $40 \div 5 = n$ OR think of this as multiplication: 5 pieces of candy in each bag × the number of bags = 40, so the correct equations to solve are $40 \div 5 = n$; $5 \times n = 40$.

4. Answer: B
Explanation: 2 rows + 3 rows = 5 rows; 5 rows × 5 equals 25.

5. Answer: C
Explanation: First, add the money she made $16 + 29 = \$45$, then subtract the money she spent $45 - 15 = \$30$.

6. Answer: D
Explanation: First, you have to find the total number of muffins, which is $4 \times 11 = 44$. Then you have to subtract the number eaten to find the total, which is $44 - 2 = 42$. Then, to find the number Sarah shared with each of her friends, you must do $42 \div 6 = 7$.

7. Answer: B
Explanation: $8 \times n = 56$ or $56 \div 8 = n$. If there are 56 legs total and Gary drew 8 legs on each spider, think 8 × what number = 56.

8. Answer: C
Explanation: $(60 - 19) \div 7$ First, subtract to find the number of pages remaining. $60 - 19$, then divide by 7 to find how many pages she needs to read each day.

9. Answer: Mia
Explanation: Max has 28 books because 4 groups of 7 is $4 \times 7 = 28$. Mia has 30 books because 5 stacks of 6 is $5 \times 6 = 30$. So, Mia has more books.

10. Answer: A
Explanation: There are 12 books on each shelf. And there are 4 shelves. So, the total books are 12 × 2.
12 can be written as 12 × 2.
So the equation can be written as
12 × 2 × 2 = 24 × 2.

11. Answer: C
Explanation: She watches TV for 35 × 6 minutes. It can be expressed as 70 × 3 as 6 can be split into 2 and 3 and 35 times 2 is 70.

12. Answer: B
Explanation: June has homework in 3 subjects, and she spends 30 minutes on each subject. She spends 90 minutes completing her homework each day. She completes 90 minutes of homework for 2 days, which means she completes 180 minutes of homework.

13. Answer: A
Explanation: There are 3 boxes with 20 sheets, and 2 boxes with 30 sheets. The total is 120 sheets. 3 × 20 = 60 and 2 × 30 = 60.
60 + 60 = 120.

14. Answer:D
Explanation: Four boxes have 120 markers. 4 × 30 = 120 markers. 2 boxes have 20 markers. 2 × 20 = 40 markers.
So, he buys 120 + 40 = 160 markers in total.

15. Answer: A
Explanation: The total number of pages read is 24 + 69 + 44 = 137.
She has to read 300 − 167 = 163 pages more.

16. Answer: Answers may vary
Explanation: Start by adding one's place. 8 + 4 is 12. One ten from 12 will carry forward to tens place. Now add all tens place. Then add all hundreds of places.

17. Answer: $216
Explanation: Six people had $ 30 (6 × $30 = $180 total) and they also each received $6 (6 × $6 = $36 total). The total amount of money is $180 + $36 = $216.

18. Answer: 40 minutes
Explanation: If the amount of time is rounded to the nearest ten minutes, he exercises for 240 minutes. When you split or divide 240 into 6 equal groups, each group will get 40.

19. Answer: B
Explanation: The number line is divided into sixths. Two-sixth or $\frac{1}{3}$ is identified by the point on this number line.

20. Answer: C
Explanation: 2 out of the 5 parts are shaded so the fraction that represents the shaded part is $\frac{2}{5}$.

21. Answer: D
Explanation: 4 out of the 8 parts are shaded so the fraction that represents the shaded part is $\frac{4}{8}$.

22. Answer:D
Explanation: Equivalent fractions are generated by multiplying the original fraction by another fraction which is equal to 1.

23. Answer: $\frac{4}{1}$
Explanation: A fraction $\frac{a}{1}$ represents the whole number a.

24. Answer: A
Explanation: Model A represents $\frac{3}{8}$ and Model B represents $\frac{5}{8}$.

25. Answer: D
Explanation: Model A represents $\frac{2}{5}$ and Model B represents $\frac{2}{4}$.

26. Answer: C
Explanation: The fraction $\frac{2}{10}$ is equivalent to $\frac{1}{5}$

27. Answer: D
Explanation: The distance between the park and Barack's school is greater distance. $\left(\frac{3}{5} > \frac{2}{5}\right)$.

28. Answer: B
Explanation: The perimeter of the figure can be determined by adding all the side lengths.

29. Answer: A
Explanation: Liters are used for volume and a water bottle is heavy.

30. Answer: A
Explanation: The perimeter of the figure can be determined by adding all the side lengths.

31. Answer: A
Explanation: The fish starts at 0 inches and ends at 5 inches on the ruler. The length is 5 inches.

32. Answer: B
Explanation: To find the area of the purple shape, subtract the missing area from the area of the rectangle.

33. Answer: 32 ft
Explanation: The area can be calculated by multiplying the length and width of the rectangle.

34. Answer: The length and width are 9 inches and is 6 inches
Explanation: The rulers on the edges of the rectangle show the length is 9 inches and the width is 6 inches.

35. Answer: B
Explanation: A car key is not very long so you would need to use the smaller of the 2 units.

36. Answer: B
Explanation: This model has 5 equal parts. Each part represents one-fifth.

37. Answer: James is incorrect.
Explanation: The model does not have 3 equal parts. This is not a representation of $\frac{2}{3}$.

38. Answer:

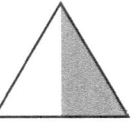 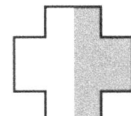

Explanation: Both the rectangle and circle should be divided into 2 equal parts, with 1 part shaded.

39. Answer: $\frac{3}{7}$
Explanation: There are 7 equal size parts in the whole. Three shaded parts represents $\frac{3}{7}$.

40. Answer:

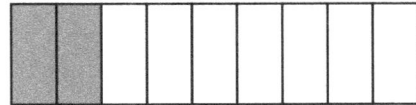

Explanation: The rectangle can be divided into 9 equal parts. The unit fraction is represented by shading 2 of the 9 equal parts.

41. Answer: No, We don't agree with Mercy.
Explanation: Two of the fractions are unit fractions ($\frac{1}{4}$ and $\frac{1}{5}$). The fractions $\frac{4}{5}$ is not a unit fraction. A unit fraction represents one part of a whole that has been divided into equal parts.

42. Answer: 8
Explanation: A model with a unit fraction of $\frac{1}{8}$ has 8 equal parts.

43. Answer: 2
Explanation: A square has two pairs of parallel sides.

44. Answer: D
Explanation: An object – the apple – divided into 3 equally sized parts mean each part represents $\frac{1}{3}$.

45. Answer: Answers may vary
Explanation: The shaded part of this model represents 2 part out of 8 equally sized parts.

COMPREHENSIVE ASSESSMENT 2

1. Answer: B
Explanation: Since one pack has 7 toys, you would need to divide 35 by 7 to find the number of packs.
35 ÷ 7 = 5 packs.

2. Answer: A
Explanation: The number line is divided into fourths. The point represents one – fourth.

3. Answer: D
Explanation: 4 rows + 2 rows = 6 rows;
6 rows × 6 equals 36.

4. Answer: B
Explanation: The model Ryker creates represents ninths. One –ninth was shaded.

5. Answer: B
Explanation: The keywords in this question are "leaving school". Kate practiced in the afternoon.

6. Answer: C
Explanation: Counting by sixes to 63 is the same as counting groups of 7 to 63;
7 × n = 63 or 63 ÷ 7 = n. 7 × 9 = 63 so Paul counted by sixes 9 times to get to 63 on the number line.

7. Answer: D
Explanation: The student recognizes $\frac{3}{7}$ and $\frac{6}{14}$ have the same number. This makes the equivalent fraction

8. Answer: C
Explanation: 5 + 5 + 5 + 5 shows adding five 4 times. Counting 5, 4 times is the same as multiplying 4×5 because there are 4 groups of 5.

9. Answer: C
Explanation: If Devin shares 8 cookies with 9 friends, think of this as 9 groups of 8 cookies. To find the total number of cookies Devin had to share, multiply 9 × 8 = 72 or use the related division fact: 72 cookies divided by 9 friends means they each get 8 cookies.
72 ÷ 9 = 8.

10. Answer: A
Explanation: 36 cookies divided into 9 bags is 36 ÷ 9, so to solve these using factors, think 9 × 4 = 36, because 36 ÷ 9= 4.

11. Answer: C
Explanation: First find a number of minutes in 7 hrs by multiplying 60 and 8. 60 × 8 = 480. Now add the 45 minutes to find the answer. 480 + 45 = 525.

12. Answer: D
Explanation: The shape is covered by squares with an area of 1 square units. There are 8 squares total.

13. Answer: B
Explanation: One – fourth is equivalent to $\frac{4}{16}$.

14. Answer: C
Explanation: 15 × 4 = (10 × 4) + (5 × 4). 14 can split into 10+5. Multiply each addend by 4, then add the product together. 15 is not being changed but split into addends that equal 15.

15. Answer:A
Explanation: 785 is 35 away from 800 and 85 away from 700. It is closer to 800.

16.Answer: C
Explanation: $\frac{7}{1}$ means dividing 7 into groups of 1. So, you will get 7 groups.

17. Answer: D
Explanation: 179 ≈ 180, 71 ≈ 70 and 58 ≈ 60 so to estimate the number of meals sold you must add 180 + 70 + 60 which is about 310.

18. Answer: A
Explanation: $(54 - 4) \div 10$ First takes the 54 slices and subtract the 4 she ate, $54 - 4$. Then divide the remaining slices by 10 $(54 - 4)$ must be completed first, then $\div\ 10$.

19. Answer: B
Explanation: The figure can be covered without any gaps or overlaps by 13 unit squares which means the area of the shape is 13 square units.

20. Answer: B
Explanation: Two raindrops have a minimal capacity. Milliliters would be the best choice for describing volume.

21. Answer: B
Explanation: The area of the rectangle can be determined by multiplying the length and width.

22. Answer: D
Explanation: The model shows 4 groups with 2 stars in each group. Count 2 stars 4 times or multiply 4×2.

23. Answer: A
Explanation: The perimeter of a rectangle can be found by 2× adding the lengths.

24. Answer: A
Explanation: 20 beads on 4 necklaces mean there are 80 beads for a total.

25. Answer: B
Explanation: Four packages of 30 cups is 5×30, or 150 cups total.

26. Answer: C
Explanation: The number line shows fourths. The point marks $\frac{3}{4}$.

27. Answer: A
Explanation: $\frac{1}{3}$ cup is a larger quantity than $\frac{1}{4}$.

28. Answer: 188 pages.
Explanation: To find the number of pages Nick read, subtract the pages yet to read 222from the total number of pages in the book, 300. Total pages Liam read is 300 - 222 = 78. Similarly subtract 190 from 300 to find the pages Sophia read. 300 - 190 = 110. Now add 78 and 110 to find the total number of pages they read. 78 + 110 = 188 pages.

29. Answer: Grace is incorrect.
Explanation: The fraction $\frac{2}{6}$ is less than $\frac{4}{8}$. Grace assumed because the first column in both fraction models is shaded that the fractions are equivalent.

30. Answer: Answers may vary
Explanation: Answers may vary. The fraction $\frac{3}{9}$ is equivalent to $\frac{1}{3}, \frac{3}{9}, \frac{6}{18}$, etc.

31. Answer: Eden is incorrect.
Explanation: A model showing $\frac{2}{3}$ should have 3 equal parts with 2 parts shaded.

32. Answer: Answers may vary
Explanation: Students should have 7 groups with 2 objects in each group.

33. Answer:

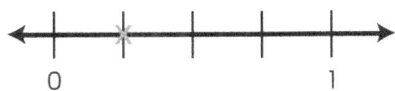

Explanation: The first hashmark after 0 represents the fraction $\frac{1}{4}$.

34. Answer: $112
Explanation: First find the perimeter of the room since she wants to border around the room. The perimeter can be found by adding all 4 sides, 8 + 20 + 8 + 20 = 56 feet. So, it would cost 56 × $2 = $112.

35. Answer: Answers may vary
Explanation: The equation $6 \times d = 42$ would help us find out how many days Rebecca did push-ups.

36. Answer: 9 square centimeters
Explanation: The area of a square (rectangle) can be determined by multiplying the side lengths.

37. Answer: Answers may vary
Explanation: 9 × 9 can help you solve 9 8 because if you know 9 × 9 is 81, then subtract a group of 9. 81 − 9 = 72 to get the product of 9×8 because 8 groups of 9 are one less group of 9 than 9 groups of 9.

38. Answer: 6 jumps 6 × 8 = 48
Explanation: 6 jumps of 8 are needed to reach 48 because 6 × 8 = 48.

39. Answer: 49 square feet
Explanation: The area of a square can be determined by multiplying the length of one side by itself.

40. Answer: 7 inches
Explanation: The hot dog starts at 7 and ends at 7 inches on the ruler.

41. Answer: 10 teams
Explanation: To find the number of teams first you must do 10+30 = 40 to find the total number of children. Then you must do 40÷4 = 10 to find the number of teams needed.

42. Answer: Array should have 5 rows of 8 or 8 rows of 5
Explanation: The expression is equivalent to 5(8) or 40. This can be determined using the distributive property.

43. Answer: $250
Explanation: The area of the room is 25 square feet and the cost per square foot of carpet is $10. 25 × 10 = 250.

44. Answer: 1
Explanation: The trapezoid has one pair of opposite parallel sides. One part is shaded.

45. Answer: Noah is correct.
Explanation: The model shows 7 equal parts. One part is shaded.